Thanks for your interest.
I look forward to
meeting you at

QLSLIVE.COM

Chris Pie

# Praise for *Real Estate on Your Terms*

*"I've known Chris for over twenty years as a business associate, client, and friend. I've seen his struggles and successes, his victories and defeats. Most importantly I have seen him grow as a person, a husband, a father, a friend, and a businessperson. His remarkable rebound story is an example of what can be accomplished when you have the will to win, the courage to be your best, and the honesty to truly assess your position in life ... and then go out and do something about it!*

*"Most importantly, Chris walks the talk. He is accountable, disciplined, and remarkably resilient. Whether you are seeking guidance in the real estate sales arena as a facilitator or as an investor, there is no better guide for you than Chris Prefontaine. All you have to do is look up the definition of* champion *in the dictionary; that's where you will find what Chris epitomizes and what you will become when you work with him."*

—V. John Alexandrov
*attorney, international best-selling author, coach*

*"Chris Prefontaine knows, and for that matter, so does the entire Prefontaine family, what it means to do the work that has to be done to reach the goal. Unlike other 'successful' people who pull up the ladder when they 'get theirs,' Chris measures success by how high he can elevate everyone around him by sharing what he has learned."*

—Jay F. Theise, Esq.

"Chris Prefontaine is an amazing entrepreneur and a man for which I have tremendous respect. I have had the pleasure of working with him over the past fifteen years. He is a man of integrity, and he seeks to help others and build relationships that last. This book is eye opening, and Chris describes what he knows best … teaching others how to win. I highly recommend this book and hope that you will take his lesson and message to heart."

—Joseph Land
*JL Capital Group, LLC*

"I've known Chris Prefontaine since grade school. He knows his stuff and has a knack for encouraging while educating people. He was a mentor to me and helped increase my residual income."

—Darren LaCroix
*CSP, AS, 2001 World Champion of Public Speaking*

"Chris has been a client and friend for close to twenty years and a business partner for ten years. We own a building in Illinois together. I'm also an investor of Chris's, stemming from him coming to interview our law firm when he moved to the area in 2004. One of the most disciplined and hardest-working people I know, he is the ultimate entrepreneur. The advice in his book comes from years of hard-won, practical experience. Pay attention and never give up."

—Richard Sayer, Esq.
*Sayer Regan & Thayer, Newport, RI*

"Real Estate on Your Terms *is filled with practical, workable methods for anyone wanting to build consistent sustainable cash flow and long-term wealth. Chris Prefontaine lays out a simple plan and implements a specific system that, when put into action, will be very profitable for novice and experienced investors alike.*

*"I've experienced firsthand the value of Chris's methods in action through his mentoring and closing highly profitable deals. If you're looking for results,* Real Estate on Your Terms *is packed full of proven techniques and I would encourage anyone looking for financial freedom to read Chris's book."*

—Don Strickland
*owner, Structure Property Solutions*

*"An outstanding resource for anyone who wants to have success in the world of real estate investing and move onward to that next level. Chris shares his real-world perspectives gained from over twenty-five years of experience as a practitioner, investor, and industry expert. Chris has coached more than thirty thousand people and has been part of $75 million worth of deals. And now in this book, Chris masterfully dissects the nine steps you need in order to become your own master transaction engineer. This is quite a masterpiece and is well needed in the marketplace. You will do deals after reading Chris's book."*

—Stephen Woessner
*CEO of Predictive ROI and host of the top-rated Onward Nation podcast*

*"In his book Chris tells a compelling story on how to invest in real estate with less risk and better cash flow than the conventional process of buy and hold or property flips. If, like many, you are concerned with the risks of investing in the stock market or regular real estate, this book could change your perspective—a worthy read."*

—Paul Dion
*CPA, CTC*

*"Whenever you can learn from mistakes, hardships, and tragedies of others, you might want to take notes. Chris Prefontaine's book,* Real Estate on Your Terms, *is an opportunity to advance. From 'lease options' to 'forced profits,' the strategies in this book are quite capable of setting one free. The question is, what do you do when life happens? Chris is a fine example of persistence and resilience. We can all stand a refresher course in that. I highly recommend you read* Real Estate on Your Terms.*"*

—Mitch Stephen
*founder of 1000houses.com and podcast host of reinvestorsummit.com*

*"Starting new ventures is filled with deep potholes and stormy economic markets; a wise man finds a guide to help. Not to worry; here is a guy to guide and nurture you step by step. Chris Prefontaine is a business builder and entrepreneur. As a coach and mentor, he is superior. Chris not only builds businesses, but he also knows how to sell and make profits and then move on to bigger and better deals.*

*"Chris is that rare, one-in-a-million person who knows 'the success formula' that you, the reader, want and need. In this text Chris does not hold back; he reveals all the information that you are searching for. He exposes his systems and formulas clearly*

*in a way the average person will understand. Chris will save you hours of frustration and show you how to avoid the pain of making big decisions, and he'll do that by following a proven and tested system. His system will result in large profits for you.*

*"Next, you need to find a comfortable chair, shut off your computer and telephone, and let your guide train and show you how to be successful in a unique business. Chris is no ivory tower professor from the university; this is a guy who comes from the trenches of work. Expect no hype, just great business stuff that will get you to the bank with deposits. In a simple chapter-after-chapter planned process, Chris is going to transform, teach, guide, and nurture you through his formula of special success. Chris has created a proven, successful moneymaking program. You'll be learning from a professional, and your small investment in time will bring you astonishing rewards."*

—Ted Thomas
*tax lien certificate and tax deed authority, www.tedthomas.com*

*"I've known Chris since freshman year of college, when he used to go home on weekends to work in his family business. He was unbelievably focused and disciplined at age eighteen, balancing work, spending time with Kim, and getting his schoolwork done. He was like a thirty-year-old businessman living among a bunch of partying college kids. He hasn't changed. He is the most driven and focused person I know! If you are interested in any aspect of the real estate business, I would highly recommend working with and learning from Chris. Learn from his tremendous knowledge and experience, and put yourself in the best position to succeed!"*

—Robert E. Romano
*estate planning attorney and real estate investor*

# REAL
# ESTATE
## ON
*your terms*

REVISED EDITION

with Bonus Chapters by Nick Prefontaine and Zachary Beach

CHRIS PREFONTAINE

# REAL ESTATE

## ON

*your terms*

CREATE CONTINUOUS CASH FLOW NOW,
WITHOUT USING YOUR CASH OR CREDIT

*Advantage*®

Copyright © 2020 by Chris Prefontaine.

All rights reserved. No part of this book may be used or reproduced in any manner whatsoever without prior written consent of the author, except as provided by the United States of America copyright law.

Published by Advantage, Charleston, South Carolina.
Member of Advantage Media Group.

ADVANTAGE is a registered trademark, and the Advantage colophon is a trademark of Advantage Media Group, Inc.

Printed in the United States of America.

10 9 8 7 6 5 4 3 2

ISBN: 978-1-64225-204-0
LCCN: 2020914951

Cover design by Katie Biondo.

This publication is designed to provide accurate and authoritative information in regard to the subject matter covered. It is sold with the understanding that the publisher is not engaged in rendering legal, accounting, or other professional services. If legal advice or other expert assistance is required, the services of a competent professional person should be sought.

Advantage Media Group is proud to be a part of the Tree Neutral® program. Tree Neutral offsets the number of trees consumed in the production and printing of this book by taking proactive steps such as planting trees in direct proportion to the number of trees used to print books. To learn more about Tree Neutral, please visit **www.treeneutral.com.**

Advantage Media Group is a publisher of business, self-improvement, and professional development books. We help entrepreneurs, business leaders, and professionals share their Stories, Passion, and Knowledge to help others Learn & Grow. Do you have a manuscript or book idea that you would like us to consider for publishing? Please visit **advantagefamily.com** or call **1.866.775.1696.**

*To my wife, Kim, for sticking with me through all the ups and downs, the goods and bads. It is certainly true that behind every good man is an amazing wife. I couldn't have done it without her. Heck, she has stuck with me for thirty-four years as of the writing of this book!*

*To my son, Nick, who watched firsthand through the 2008–2012 transition, and to my daughter, Kayla, and Kayla's husband, Zach, who joined the biz in 2016. As of the writing of this book, they have grown into pivotal roles and are more than capable of running the entire business for the many decades ahead.*

*To our amazing team at the office and spread around the world who help, assist, and support in every way and who put up with me nonstop!*

Please note that Chris Prefontaine or Chew Publishing, Inc. DBA/ SmartRealEstateCoach.com earnings are in no way average and that any examples provided should not be considered typical, as your results will vary depending on many factors. If you think you can get rich by simply clicking a button or allowing others to do all the work, then we recommend you do not invest your money in any educational program or business tool, as it will not be a good investment. Our team is here to support you, and we hope that you make buying decisions because you are also dedicated to success.

From time to time we send emails promoting other companies' products or services and may earn commission for doing so. It is important to realize that while we only send products, services, or events that we believe will help your business and that we've trialed, we do not recommend investing in anything without doing your own due diligence. As with anything in life, in order to succeed you will need to put forth effort and be persistent. And finally, any information provided is educational and cannot be taken as legal or financial advice.

# contents

# *foreword*

## *by Mitch Stephen*

If you had asked the young Mitch Stephen to envision what his life and business would look like today, I guarantee you I never would've described anything close to what my reality is now. The financial freedom and flexibility I enjoy because of my real estate business would have seemed unfathomable at the starting line twenty-four years ago. After doing the math, here's where things stand: I've bought a property in or about my hometown of San Antonio, Texas, every four to five days, for over two decades! That's over two thousand properties since 1996. And because of the systems and team we have in place, I haven't even seen the last four hundred houses we've bought, nor have I ever met the last four hundred people who bought my properties. I just see the details on the spreadsheet. It took me way too long to develop those systems and become a true owner of a real company.

Chris invited me to write this foreword because he knows my backstory and that none of what I just described happened by accident or luck. I definitely did not come from money or even an entrepreneurial bloodline. I was given nothing and rose from the dirt. What I did have was a terrific mother and father who taught me right from wrong. They gave me a great work ethic and never told me, "You can't." They always told me, "You can!" I'm very sure that created the right belief system and mindset. I added the grit and the willingness to find my place in the world. I found it in real estate.

Once I realized I had a passion for real estate investing, I started listening to those who had already done what I wanted to do. I started doing what they were doing. I did the same things over and over and over again, but a little bigger, a little better, and a little faster each time. That's how you systematize, scale, and create financial freedom.

When you're looking for your first several deals, it can be hard to envision what success looks like. You need to mentally bridge the gap between where you are now and where you want to be. And while you're doing that, all sorts of fears, worries, and doubts will try to creep in. You might even hear that little voice in your head telling you that success is not for you. You have to combat that voice. You fight that voice by getting in front of evidence that proves that voice wrong. Dead wrong!

Remember Roger Bannister? He was the British middle-distance athlete and neurologist who ran the first sub-four-minute mile. No one believed that running a mile in less than four minutes could be done. It was considered ... impossible. Then, one day, Roger did it! He broke the four-minute mark. And once Roger had proved it possible, other runners believed they could do it—and they did. Roger had shifted their mindsets and helped them bridge the gap so they could see the possibilities.

I've taken that same lesson and applied it to my real estate business. Over the last twenty-four years, I attended mastermind groups and joined communities where investors shared their success stories and showed their tax returns as real evidence. I got into places where that voice of negativity could not even begin to compete with the positivity I was seeing. It was powerful, and it dramatically shifted my perception. It helped me bridge the gap because I could see with real confirmation what was possible and how they did it. I wasn't guessing or estimating anymore. I was doing what had been proven to work for others before me. Confirmation that it could be done and that it was being done led me to one solid conclusion: "If they can do it, I can do it!"

With that evidence, I could see myself applying the same steps with similar success. I left each session energized, with new things to try and a set of decisions to be made around how to raise the expectations for my business.

My hope for you is that Chris's book and his Quantum Leap System (QLS) will provide the same confirmation and help you bridge the same gaps in your own business so you can see what's possible.

Look, I know what it feels like to be broker than broke. I also know what it feels like to be uncertain about what steps to take next. I'm telling you, everything you need in order to feel certain, to change your financial circumstances by doing terms deals, or to scale your real estate business even further is here in this book and within QLS. Nothing has been hidden or left out.

As it was for me, your biggest obstacle to success will likely be your current belief system and mindset. If you think small, you will play small. If you allow yourself to change your belief system to thinking bigger, then you will play that way. Your world will begin to change. You will meet the right coaches and mentors who can help you bridge the gap so you can scale your business with the right systems, delegation, and automation. And then you will have everything you need to build a business that provides you and your family with financial freedom and flexibility.

You just need to take that first step. And then someday I'll read about your two thousand deals. I look forward to that!

# *foreword*

## *by Scott Ulmer*

Ever driven down a country road, glanced over, and noticed, in the middle of a crowded cornfield, one stalk sticking out above the rest? Every once in a while, someone crosses your path who catches your eye and grabs your attention—who "sticks out" from the crowd and, for reasons you are not quite sure of at first, leaves a lasting imprint on you. Whatever "it" is, they seem to have it. Their qualities and characteristics leave you without a glimmer of doubt that they are destined to achieve great success in whatever their endeavor.

It was in 2013 that Chris Prefontaine and I crossed paths. I had the distinct pleasure of working with him as he and countless others rebuilt the lives and financial success they had prior to the devastation the 2008 market crash brought.

It was clear from the outset that Chris stuck out above the rest. His sense of focus and purpose-driven approach to life, combined with his Rhode Island twang, made it a pleasure to connect with him every week. And to see the success he achieved in such a short time was a true pleasure for me.

It was evident he was a superstar from the first time we chatted. He epitomized everything a high-level performer has, and in no time at all he was back to crushing his real estate deals, rebuilding the empire he had built once before, only this time he would build it stronger and battle hardened. To this day I consider him a friend, and every time we talk, I glean another "nugget of gold" from him.

But for Chris it wasn't just rising from the proverbial ashes; he was on a mission to provide for his wife and family—to get them back the lives they had and deserved to have again. Since that time, I have had a front-row seat to his rocket ship rise back to the top. I have watched him crush the goals he set and exceed far above even his tremendously high expectations. And now you, too, the reader, have the privilege and pleasure of seeing Chris's off-the-charts comeback and the circumstances and obstacles he overcame to get there, achieving greater and fuller success than he had before.

You will hear firsthand Chris's story of restoration and the personal challenges he had to deal with in the midst of his rebuild, how he is a *master* at nontraditional and creative real estate deals, and how you, too, can emulate his success if you are tenacious and willing to put in the work, simply by following the outline he provides in this book.

Nothing in life worth having comes easy, but if you are willing to put in the time and follow directions, the following pages will outline step by step Chris's blueprint for success in real estate in today's market. You will enjoy not only hearing Chris's story but gleaning the valuable content contained within. Whether you are a seasoned real estate pro or a beginner, I promise you will have several takeaways from this insightful book.

And be sure you have a highlighter and pen close by, as your mind will be stimulated with ideas and inspiration to go out and create the life and success you deserve for you and your family.

# *acknowledgments*

This book could not have been written without the help, influence, and inspiration of many people. It's simply not possible to thank everyone who contributes to a project of this scope, but I'd like to make special mention of a few people.

First and foremost, I'd like to thank my wife, Kim, for her amazing support, encouragement, inspiration, and work on this project. The early mornings and late nights would not be possible without that very important sounding board and unending support. Second, my kids, who are now not only an integral part of our businesses but have helped with this project each step of the way: son Nick, daughter Kayla, and son-in-law Zach. I am enjoying watching your growth and applaud your own best seller, *The New Rules of Real Estate Investing: 24 Leading Experts Reveal Their Real Estate Secrets*, which we coauthored.

I'd also like to express my appreciation and admiration for all my mentors and accountability partners over the years. The ideas and brainstorms—not just for this book, but for business in general—have translated into millions of dollars directly from all of you. I cannot risk missing someone by naming individuals. You know who you are, and you are immensely appreciated.

I'd also like to express my appreciation to my parents, Bob and Lin, for their continued support with the book and everything else that I journey off to accomplish, as well as my late brother, Jay, who passed away at the young age of forty-seven and who was a writer who helped mold my writing style and habits by his never-ending editing of e-books and stories over the years. Jay, we may have never gotten the chance to write together, but your inspiration served the book very well.

Special thanks must also go to one of my attorneys, who's also my friend, Richard Sayer. Richard stood by me and encouraged me and believed in me even during the downturn.

I must also express my tremendous appreciation to Advantage Media and their numerous staff people who made this project a reality. A project of this size is made much less difficult with their kind of assistance.

# *about the authors*

**Chris Prefontaine,**
**Owner, Smart Real Estate Coach**

Chris Prefontaine is a three-time bestselling author of *Real Estate on Your Terms, The New Rules of Real Estate Investing*, and Moneeka Sawyer's *Real Estate Investing for Women*.

He's also the founder and CEO of **smartrealestatecoach.com** and host of the Smart Real Estate Coach Podcast.

Chris has been in real estate for almost thirty years. His experience ranges from constructing new homes in the 1990s and owning a Realty Executives franchise to running his own investments (commercial and residential) and coaching clients throughout North America.

Today, Chris runs his own buying and selling businesses with his family team, which purchases from two to five properties monthly, so they're in the trenches every single week. They also help their associates and students do the exact same thing all across North America, working together on another ten to fifteen properties every month.

Having been through several real estate cycles, Chris understands the challenges of this business and helps students navigate the constantly changing real estate waters.

## Zachary Beach, COO and Coach

Zachary is the Amazon best-selling author of *The New Rules of Real Estate Investing* and cohost of the *Smart Real Estate Coach Podcast*. He is a partner, COO, and coach at Smart Real Estate Coach. At

the age of twenty-five, Zach decided to leave the world of bartending and personal training and jump into the family business. It was one of the first big risks that he took in his life, as nothing was guaranteed. Plus, he knew *absolutely nothing* about real estate. Through hard work, in-house training, and implementation, Zach has now completed over one hundred deals and growing. On top of that, he coaches students around the country on how to buy and sell property just like his family still does. Now, as a group, they buy and sell ten to fifteen properties a month with a predictable and scalable system, controlling $20–$25 million worth of real estate at any one time with little to no money in the deal and no banks involved. Zach has been in the business for over four years and now runs all operations of Smart Real Estate Coach on top of continuing to coach his students and Associates. He has an amazing wife, Kayla, and two small children: his son, Remi, and his daughter, Bellamy. He is a prime example of how to be successful both in business and at home.

**Nick Prefontaine,
Partner and Coach**

In 2003, Nick was in a snowboarding accident that left him in a coma for over three weeks. The doctors told his parents that he probably wouldn't walk, talk, or eat on his own again. Less than three months later, he was running out of Franciscan Children's Hospital. Now a certified Infinite Possibilities trainer, Nick speaks to groups that benefit from his message of overcoming adversity. Nick grew up in the real estate industry and got started on his own at an early age. Most notably, he was knocking on pre-foreclosure doors at sixteen and seventeen, doing up to fifty doors a day. This experience helped shape Nick's real estate career. Now, Nick specializes in working with lease purchasers to get them into a home and on the path to home ownership. Regardless of a buyer's credit situation, he looks at their complete financial picture and comes up with a plan to get them into a home.

# prologue

Kim and I were sitting at our kitchen island in one of our homes, in Shrewsbury, Massachusetts. Our kids were in the next room, Kayla doing her homework and Nick studying his real estate material. It was February 2008, but looking back, I still vividly remember that night—I'll never forget it. Kim and I were just getting ready for dinner, and I could smell the awesome Italian meal cooking on the stove. The cars in the driveway were all brand new, as was the home. Everything was perfect, or so it appeared. But if you saw the look on my face, you would know that something was up.

You would have heard Kim say to me, "Okay, we just did the refinance; a couple hundred thousand dollars came in and out—like that. What are we going to do next month? The overall real estate market is crashing—how are we going to do this?"

We were responsible for hundreds of subcontractors and a dozen employees. We had had some amazingly profitable years together and owned twenty-three properties, some with partner-investors. The properties were all either in foreclosure, going through the foreclosure process, or in a short sale. It was a full-time job just to handle that. We had the IRS calling and sending nastygrams. Our credit cards had been shut off, sometimes without notice. Eight to ten years' worth of savings, investments, college funds, and retirement funds had been cashed out to try to survive.

I said to Kim, "What the heck were we thinking?" Our daughter, Kayla, was eighteen, finishing up in a private high school and looking forward to college. Our son, Nick, was nineteen. Refinancing our second home in Newport, Rhode Island, on two acres overlooking the harbor, was supposed to have provided enough cash ($350,000) to save our real estate company. But we had a couple of million dollars in mortgages on top of our children's education expenses. I had made the ultimate mistake of thinking the housing market was never going to stop climbing. Too many of us used our real estate holdings like an ATM machine. The cash-out we had gotten from the refinancing was a bandage that allowed us to pay expenses for our businesses temporarily but required another round of refinancing at a lower interest rate within twelve months.

Chest pains were constant with all that stress. You know how the real estate market came to a halt in 2007–2008. Property values plunged, leading to the drying up of credit. Then, in February 2008, almost as if a light switch had been thrown, financing stopped. Deal funding stopped. All large commercial deals on the books, projected to provide hundreds of thousands in profit, were dead in the water with all banks shutting down funding.

Clearly this was not real estate on *my* terms, but rather on the banks' terms.

Financing at the time was a challenge, because I had purchased buildings the conventional way—putting 10 percent or 20 percent of our money or investors' money down and signing for a loan. The goal pre-2007 had been to accumulate twenty or so properties using cash, investors, and bank loans. Then, as the market continued to rise and as we improved the properties, the plan was to sell those off at a profit. That was no longer a path to get out when market values fell by one-third to one-half in 2007. We had no safeguard against a market crash, nor did we really create any up-front or ongoing cash flow—we were focused on long-term wealth and cash-outs only. (You'll see in this book how we fixed our business's cash flow challenge by creating the **3 Paydays**.)

Before the real estate market crash, about one-third of our purchases were **commercial or mixed-use properties,** and the rest were two- to six-unit apartment buildings, half of which could become condominiums. We would work with engineers and attorneys to completely rehabilitate all the units of those multifamily buildings, convert them into condos, and resell at a nice profit, usually within a few months. The profit was fantastic until the downturn, when we got caught with four or five units that we had to rent or sell at a loss.

**3 PAYDAYS:**

1. A cash deposit from the down payment
2. Monthly cash flow
3. Back-end profit

**COMMERCIAL PROPERTIES:**

Buildings or land intended to generate a profit.

**MIXED-USE PROPERTIES:**

Building or complex that blends residential, commercial, and other property types together.

The mixed-use buildings had similar problems. One in Rhode Island, in a lower- to middle-class inner-city area, had four retail units, with four residential units above. I brought in an investor for about $200,000 but still had a $500,000 bank loan. The four commercial units—a nail salon, a beauty parlor, an office, and a window and siding retailer—were supposed to provide most of the income, but two of those went out of business with the economic downturn.

Finally, there were the buildings we kept as multifamily rentals. With no profit coming in from the other properties to fix up or even properly maintain those apartment buildings, we had no exit path from those purchases, as they were not attractive to buyers unless offered at less than what we owed, or what bankers call a **short sale**.

The banks forgave debt during the crash for some individual property owners but fought to collect from investors, although eventually they had to write off debt or settle on short sales with us.

**SHORT SALE:**
Any sale of real estate that generates profit less than the amount owed on the property.

At the time, we took a big hit. But since then, we've more than made up for losses by profiting on the many lessons learned from 2007–2008. And you, too, can learn from these lessons and avoid the same mistakes in your business.

Now that you know how I *used to* do business, forget about it—unless you want to experience the heart palpitations and the stress I endured in 2008, along with visits from tow trucks looking for a car or truck to repo or the IRS mailings that were constantly looking for money. I have told you these details because it's important for you to understand that signing personally on loans, refinancing properties for cash-out without a specific exit plan, and entering any deal whatsoever that does not create immediate and continuous cash flow are *not* good strategies. You can buy some properties and hold them, but I'll show you how to do so with both cash flow and a hedge against the market—without using your own cash or credit.

## DIGGING OUT

I didn't survive alone. With the help of a supportive wife and some great mentors, I dug my business out of the hole over the ensuing five years. But it wasn't easy. I remember one friend, Cle, a successful builder and business owner from Massachusetts, telling me in 2008, "It could take you ten years. It could take you five. Whatever it's going to take, you communicate with people. You be open with them. You let them know what's going on. The whole nation is dealing with this. You be the one who speaks up and communicates well, and remember, you didn't personally take down the national real estate market!" I never forgot that. That helped me a lot when dealing with the creditors, vendors, and investors, and I've reminded him a few times and thanked him.

Numerous attorneys and friends said, "You should just file for bankruptcy. To heck with everyone." I didn't want to do that. We painfully went through setting up payment plans with creditors, vendors, and banks as necessary. The communications involved taught me many lessons we'll discuss throughout the book and that I use in coaching new investors and partners. If you're seeking a mentor or a coach and they have not experienced any downturns, run. They simply won't know how to navigate. I've experienced three and have the bruises to show so that you can minimize or eliminate yours. (You'll see how I became passionate about helping others learn from my experience—the impetus for this book.)

At a certain point, I had to resume the focus on creating cash flow, which would be the real key to satisfying the creditors as well as getting ourselves back on our feet. I committed to spend half of each day moving on to new business. I set standards for that new business:

- no more personal signing for loans

- constant communication with mentors and coaches

- making sure we bought only properties that could be obtained without using our own cash or credit

I call these standards buying and selling on YOUR TERMS. As of this writing, we control fifty-five to sixty or more properties (pending cash-outs), mostly single-family residential homes of our own, and then another fifty or so with Associates throughout North America. We either have title or control them through a **lease-pur-chase** or other agreement. But each month we are taking on new properties (or owner financing or subject to existing financing) and cashing some out.

This book will explain in detail, with actual numbers, how buying and selling on YOUR TERMS works for the seller, the buyer,

**LEASE-PURCHASE AGREEMENT:**

A contract in which a portion of the lease payment or rent is applied to the purchase price of the property.

and us as a family business, and how we structure these deals on our own terms with the parameters of not using our own cash, not taking out a bank loan, and not risking our credit.

Buying and selling on terms is the opposite of what I did from 2004 through 2008. I credit one of my initial mentors, whom I met in 2005 at his ninety-nine-dollar seminar that a friend invited me to. I was hesitant to go, because my wife and I had been on a great run in real estate since 1991 and were not looking for something new. We had built more than one hundred single-family homes, then bought a Realty Executives franchise for all of Central New England in 1994. Despite mentors telling me "you cannot sell a real estate brokerage business," we sold it to Coldwell Banker in 2000 for a quarter of a million dollars and then started coaching other real estate agents around the United States and Canada. Our team—consisting of one agent (me), one full-time assistant, and a runner for signs and miscellaneous personal errands—had been doing more than a hundred transactions per year. We had fifteen affiliated agents averaging more than twenty transactions per year, five to ten times the national average. Having worked with real estate agents unhappily at first as a builder, I understood the standards we needed to establish to be successful.

## COACHING YOU TO MAKE CASH NOW
## AND IMPROVE CASH FLOW

You may be wondering, *Do I have to be a licensed real estate agent to buy and sell property on terms?* I will go into this in more detail in chapter 3, but the short answer is that if you buy property under your name or your company name and then resell that property, you're acting on your own behalf, and you're not conducting a service for a fee, so *no license is required.*

I'm not a lawyer or a licensing expert, so you should consult a local attorney because state laws vary. You have to be careful to have the proper paperwork and the proper structure to comply with state and local licensing guidelines.

Buying and selling on YOUR TERMS asks you to study and train to transact the kinds of deals described in this book. There's a lot of information you won't be able to absorb all at once. But beyond this book, we provide tools, such as **Smart Real Estate Coach Academy** (that's where our staple foundational product lives—Quantum Leap System Video Program, referred to as QLS Video Program, as well as other training programs); our unique **Associate Program**, whereby we actually do deals with individuals around North America and revenue share with them as part of our consulting; and our two annual events—**Quantum Leap System Live Event** (referred to as QLS Live Event) and **Business Scaling Secrets Event.** You can register for these on our website.

Our Associate Program helps you immerse yourself in the learning that is one of three major factors for long-term success. The second factor is having the right tools, which our QLS Video Program provides—from live-deal videos, family team lesson videos, and live calls with buyers and sellers to the proper vendors and resources you'll need. The third factor is having us hands-on walking you through a successful deal from the lead generated to a check in your hand. Unfortunately, I've come to learn that there is an enormous gap in the industry. This gap is the time between someone studying a course or attending an event and then actually doing a deal. For some, this gap is never overcome. Our Academy, as well as our Associate Program, has shortened—even eliminated for some—that gap. If you're stuck in that gap and have spent money to get into that gap, forget that—it has no bearing on your future success.

Our family business is based in New England but is expanding much farther, because our ideas and the Associate Program are working across North America. We are helping our Associates realize the same averages as our private family company for per-deal profits with all 3 Paydays of $75,000 (for our deals) and $45,000 to $200,000 for all our Associates on average—depending upon the type of transaction and where they are geographically. Those profits aren't guarantees, of course, and results can vary for myriad reasons, but readers of this book will learn how they're possible for sure. Some come to us with zero experience and others with years of experience in a different niche.

For example, we work with a man who has a full-time job as an engineer in Pennsylvania but wants to transition into real estate investing. Within ninety days we helped him into his first deal, which will gross him $66,111 over twenty-four months. On our website you can see how he describes, in his own words, spending years "playing around" with real estate by attending disappointing seminars and "failed attempts with some mentors." In a testimonial letter he sent—accompanying a copy of his first lease-purchase check after he started working with us—he said, "I jumped in not knowing what I was doing with some seller calls, but I thought, 'What's the worst that's going to happen? They'll say no and hang up.' It was quite the contrary, as many of the sellers were very pleasant to talk to, and your scripts, videos, etc. on your website helped ... If someone would have told me that I could make over $66k on a $130k house, I would have told them they're crazy!" His enthusiasm didn't wane, and he sent a second testimonial letter when he made his second and third deals, in the same week: "I'm loving the $236,000 Payday with you in three deals!"

Also in Pennsylvania, there's Sean, a police detective who understandably says he has grown tired of kicking down doors at night to bust drug dealers. He wants to be home with his family more. In his first thirty days, he did a deal that will gross him more than $56,000 over three years. He recounts the details on our website and says, "Without Chris's coaching, the process would probably have seemed overwhelming, but in working with Chris, you learn to relate to people's needs and be system driven from a business perspective. It also helps that I'll pocket roughly $10,000 up front, $700 per month net income for forty-eight months, and another $20,000 or so when cashed out—I think that makes my coaching investment return quite high in relation to what I spent—not bad!"

*Sean H., police officer who made a $65,000 deal in his first thirty days by buying and selling on his terms.*

Then there's Dave P. in Michigan, who found a home so loaded with liens that the seller just wanted to give him the home. After our due diligence together and a few attorneys later, we found out all $185,000 of the liens were going to drop off in less than five years due to the statute of limitations on them. We then realized a deal in which we anticipated all 3 Paydays to be around $70,000 or so, now increased by approximately $185,000. You'll learn in this book how we find the most motivated sellers to work with, and this one was a good example. We structured a deal in which we purchased the home subject to the existing financing (mortgage stays in the seller's name, and we take ownership of the home).

## CASH FLOW ON YOUR TERMS

Is it worth your time to try buying and selling on YOUR TERMS? Well, you can decide after you learn in this book the value of the **3 Paydays** you receive:

1. The nonrefundable down payment up front

2. The monthly cash flow per deal, averaging $409, or about $5,000 a year on terms,[1] ranging from an average minimum three years to as much as ten years or more

3. The cash-out at the back end

A few paragraphs earlier, I mentioned the averages for the 3 Paydays, but our Paydays increase as we become more effective at managing deals and increasing profits. I call those Payday #4s, and we review them at each of our Associate Development days that precede the events we hold. Is that type of money worth your time? Well, if you do a few of those deals per year, it's more than most people make at a full-time job.

---

1    Our averages at time of writing.

If you tend to be skeptical, take a closer look at the real stories throughout this book and on the website, because yes, it does work in your market and in your price range.

This book explains what we mean by YOUR TERMS and why buyers and sellers will want to work with you once you become a master **transaction engineer**, using the Nine Steps to Success that I will show you. We'll discuss the types of profitable deals you can make in real estate without risking your own money and how to do them in a simple, proven, and predictable way. You'll learn the systems necessary to generate the right leads in your area and how to convert them—simultaneously—to cash NOW, monthly cash flow, and wealth building for the future.

**TRANSACTION ENGINEER:**

Someone who has mastered the Nine Steps to Success and is ready to do deals. A transaction engineer is able to look at a property-information sheet, debrief a seller, structure the right deal, and then place it in the right bucket.

---

**Note to readers:** For many readers of this book, making their own terms may involve learning some new terminology. So each real estate and banking term will be defined in a box alongside the text.

---

# THRIVING IN CHAOS

I don't know when we'll be coming out of this COVID-19 virus situation, but I do feel it would be a disservice not to address how it affects our niche. I've worked incredibly hard to build a system and a coaching mechanism as well as products that get us as close to recession resistant as possible. Today, in the current climate dealing with the virus and everything that comes with it, I brought to the Wicked Smart Community via our podcast (**smartrealestatecoachpodcast.com**) a special four-episode series titled *Thriving in Chaos*. You can and should go review those as well as subscribe so you don't miss any future episodes. That very important and timely message, as well as this bonus chapter, is to help you through these extraordinary times.

Will this be the last time we deal with this situation?

Will something similar come again?

I'm the ultimate optimist, but if you look at the history books, every 80 to 120 years, a major crisis or shift has happened.

Now, unfortunately, I'm fully aware that many people in the world are hurting right now, and some of you may be among them. I understand that, and we want to help. Others are very fortunate right now to be thriving. Amazon comes to mind (they just hired over a hundred thousand people), as well as other online niches like that and companies like Home Depot, pet stores, and more. In fact, as of the day I'm writing this chapter, we have two buyers who have applied for one of our rent-to-own homes. Both work for Home Depot, and both are super busy taking on overtime and making more than they're used to.

Our niche certainly is booming right now. We want to help you help others who aren't as fortunate. Many people in the world need a sanity check to help them act boldly, to help them in this unprecedented market shift. We want to help you there as well. And specifically, we want to help lead you through the current crisis (or future if it's in our rearview mirror as of the time of this printing) to a better tomorrow, to help you literally find a way to thrive during the chaos.

We're going to be guiding you through the best way to take control over your own life through real estate specifically and how to thrive during this chaos. As banks clamp down on loans and raise the bar for qualifying criteria, more and more buyers and sellers need us. This reminds me of 2012 and 2013, before things started to improve. The important thing to remember about the terms business is that it works well in all markets.

Now, I know that for many of you, this idea of just controlling your own life, or even the word *thriving*, may seem a little far fetched, a little out there. That's precisely why we wanted to include this chapter—to help give you specific, actionable steps to take control back and to thrive. For those of you who are fortunate enough to be thriving already or in our Wicked Smart Community and thriving, we hope you'll pull some interesting nuggets out while feeling proud to be part of this niche! We understand there are different niches, and there are extremes out there in the marketplace right now—it doesn't seem there are any happy mediums right now. We'd like to help you do two things.

First and foremost, spread that positive energy, spread that knowledge, spread that know-how and guidance to others who want and need it. Second, take that positivity and parlay that situation in order to go out and help tens of thousands of buyers and sellers. We can do that right now. That's a superpositive thing we have going on for us in this niche. This is what I call the Perfect Triangle:

## PERFECT TRIANGLE

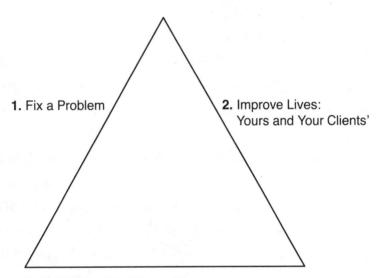

**1.** Fix a Problem

**2.** Improve Lives:
Yours and Your Clients'

**3.** Get Paid to Do #1 and #2
We Don't Just Want Good: It's a Movement,
It's a Family, It's Outstanding.
**Who Do You Want to Become This Decade?**

We're part of a movement always and forever with the Wicked Smart Community. More than ever we can help so many buyers and sellers, and as a result, we get paid very well to do so—the Perfect Triangle.

I do believe part of the necessary growth, lessons, and proper guidance from all this comes from information, so we're going to share some information to help you make better decisions. Part of it also comes from encouragement, and as any longtime listeners of our podcast, readers of our books, or members of the Wicked Smart Community know, we are your biggest cheerleaders. Lastly, part of it also comes from experience and a creative perspective, so we want to give you that experience, and we want to give you that creative perspective always.

When this chaos really started to kick in, my wife asked me, "How will this affect your business? How is this going to affect your Associates? How's it going to affect your buyers and sellers?"

She was genuinely concerned, probably more so than I was at the time. I hadn't really taken it all in yet. I don't have a crystal ball. Full disclosure: I'm not an economist, so let's be super clear there before we go further. What I did say to her was more along these lines:

"I don't know yet. Let me digest it and get a feel for how things affect our buyers, our sellers, and our students. But one thing is for sure," I said to her, "and I want you to hear this loud and clear: Wicked Smart Community cannot change what's going on, but we can most definitely react the way we choose to, knowing full well that someday, whether that's a few weeks, a few days, a few months, a year, things will start moving back to normal."

Let's now think about what I call the center line. We can be behind the center line after this is all over, playing catch-up. We can be just at the center line, getting by and being ready. Or we can be way ahead of the center line. The important part to know here is that we have that choice. We can control that. You can control that.

I then went on to remind Kim that we've been through a lot since we got married thirty-four years ago. I'm going to date myself here!

We've been married since 1986, and here's what we've gone through:

- I was fired in 1991 from a company that purchased my father's company after I had been working there for about a month. My kids were going on two and going on three years of age. I had bought our first home literally months before and was 100 percent out of a job.

- In 1993, after building a business for two years, just coming off being fired with a partner of mine building single-family homes, I got a call from my attorney, who basically said, "You've been pushed into involuntary bankruptcy by your creditors." Now, first of all, I didn't even know what that meant. Second of all, I was twenty-six or twenty-seven years old and had no idea how to navigate that.

- We were all hit by 9/11, like everyone else. I was stuck in Italy with Kim. We had a business to run at home, and our kids were at home.

- In 2003 I got another one of those chaotic phone calls, those surprise phone calls, that basically said, "Your son was in a snowboard accident. He's in a coma. He can't be airlifted to the hospital because it's too windy, so we've had to intubate him on-site, and we're bringing him to the hospital." My life was flipped upside down.

- The 2008 debacle flipped my life upside down yet again.

- In 2013, when all that was over and I started buying homes, people said I was crazy to be buying during this time.

I could go on and on here, but I just gave you five or six major curveballs that have hit Kim and me over the years. Were any of those virus related? Nope. Not at all. But they were chaotic changes that came with challenges.

As I think back, two of those came at times when I had no mentor or no one to lean on. Big mistake, and part of the reason we are so involved with our Associates and the Wicked Smart Community is that we will always be their guide through all different economic cycles and challenges. I mentioned the 80–120-year cycle earlier in this chapter. Guess what? Eventually things pass, things change, and people get through to the other side. Some of mine that I mentioned were absolutely brutal, but we got through to the other side. And guess what? So many people got to the other side over the years, and so many got to the other side in a very positive fashion, ahead of where they had been, because of the choices they made and the guides who were with them. And that includes who they surrounded themselves with.

So no, I haven't gone through this exact chaos, but chaos isn't new to me, and I'm here to guide you. Our team at Smart Real Estate Coach is here to guide you. Literally, if you want a call with me, a private call, I want to open this up to the entire Wicked Smart Community—and I know this is going to swamp me, which I know is going to be maybe a headache—but I invite you to email my personal assistant, **kristen@smartrealestatecoach.com**, and schedule a call with me. But let her know you saw this in my book. Let's talk through your situation. Let's talk through your next best moves for your family, your business, your health, or anything else you'd like to work on. Anything else you'd like to discuss, I'd like to give you that free strategy call.

Here's what I know: As humans, we've all heard of and experienced, of course, the underlying fight-or-flight instincts. There's a third very scary one, and it's called freeze. I don't care what niche in real estate you're in; I don't care if you're in a different industry altogether; the worst thing you can do right now is freeze. Many did as of the time of this writing, and probably many still are. I understand that. We could have frozen. I'll give you a quick example. Just a couple of weeks before this chapter was being completed, we had an upcoming event—hotel booked, food ordered, stage ordered, cameras ordered, everything ready to go. This virus turned it upside down. We pivoted just as quickly as we could. We're not experts in this, but we pulled off a virtual event. We could have frozen. The Wicked Smart Community ended up loving the event, and we had two and a half times the audience because virtual was easier than traveling—win-win. I personally know three other big businesses in real estate training who shut down their events and just pushed them to a later date—huge mistake, in my opinion.

Realtors right now—and if you're a Realtor, please, no offense meant. Many Realtors—in fact, all whom I've interacted with—have frozen. Yes, the economy may be against you. Yes, the attorney generals may be against you for going out, but you can do other things. You can say, "How can I operate in this?"

I'm very thankful that many Realtors are calling us and referring us their sellers because they know that we can do something with them, but there is no reason to freeze.

Let's take another example, and then I'll move on: our own buying and selling, and our Associates' buying and selling. We could have all frozen. Instead, we and they are thriving more than ever—more business, more deals than ever. Why? We're asking *how*, not freezing. Now, I know it's tough. I'm not candy coating it, but you do have choices here, and there is a way. Just ask for help, and ask those questions of yourself.

Now, let me pivot. If you're feeling anxious now, or you're feeling anxious at all, or have any fear or anxiety whatsoever, I want to share with you how I chose to deal with all those curveballs since 1991. I encourage you to act on this today. When you get done with this chapter, act on these three items. I encourage you to do that anytime you feel fear or anxiety—not just because of COVID-19; anything, anytime in your life. What are the items?

1.  Let's identify the fear or anxiety. Is it actual, or is it some insecurity? Is it some insecurity maybe from the past, way back? Like a teacher, or a parent, or a friend, or a brother, or sister who affected you? Let's recognize what's going on in your head right now for the fear or anxiety. But then let's realize that that fear or anxiety could be complete bullshit once we dissect it. Now, you're not here to play small. You would not be taking the time to read this if you were.

2.  Write down, today, what's absolutely fantastic in your life right now. Just last Sunday I did this exercise. I do it often; that's why I'm sharing it with you. And I did it again this morning as I was journaling, before I even knew I was going to go ahead and write this chapter. In starting our virtual event, I outlined for people how positive it is. I said, "This is not a negative that we're not together," even though so many of the Wicked Smart Community wanted to be together—they're like family. I reminded them that they're probably saving 30 percent of the time just because they don't have to travel. I reminded them that they're probably saving 95 percent of the costs. And they're probably going to network a whole bunch more because we have breakout

rooms and all kinds of cool things going on virtually in Zoom. That's what I mean by segregating what's fantastic right now in your life versus what we could have done. We could have panicked—oh, man, we had to cancel the hotel; what a headache. Oh man, we can't bring everyone in. Oh man, we better cancel the event. As I wrote earlier, I know there are mentors, teachers, educators in our space who canceled events. What a big mistake. In fact, I personally emailed one I'm sure many of you know—he's not a small name in the industry—and I said, "I think that was a mistake you canceled your event. Let me help you understand how we did our virtual events." I don't know if his ego is going to allow him to call me back, but I reached my hand out to help him. I'll give you another example of things that can be fantastic: more time with family right now. My coach, Jaireck Robbins, Tony Robbins's son, said to me, during this chaos, among other things, "How are your relationship goals going?" And he gave me seven things to focus on. Absolutely amazing.

3. Now look to the future, one year out. Put a date on the paper right now. Change the date to one year out. Now, outline your ideal outcome. You look back, and everything's past. What's going on now that's absolutely fantastic? Create it. Here's your chance to create it. Let me give you some ideas. Let me give you some brain teasers. What kind of money's coming in? What did you create? Did you, in our niche, create 3 Paydays? If you created 3 Paydays and you bore down for the last year, then as you look back from next year to now, you would have created Paydays that are somewhere in the range of $45,000 to

$250,000 per deal. What's that look like? How about your family situation? How much closer did you become? What cool things did you do when you were stuck at home? How about your health?

During this time when I'm at home more, I said to my wife, "There's never been a more focused time on my health." Now, thanks to Jairek Robbins, my coach, a lot of that came from him, but it was because I had time to do it here. I had a different schedule here; everything was here at home. I'm writing this chapter at home.

These three things that I gave you can break any shitty or offbeat anxious fear or bad habit. You've got to do it constantly, though. It's like working out. You're not going to go to the gym one day and say, "Got it, feel great, changed my stomach, changed my waistline, changed my weight." No, it's going to take time, and it's going to take consistency. These three things I just gave you—identifying the fear, writing down what's absolutely fantastic, and then creating your best year ever by looking back one year—that's what you have to do on a regular basis. Now and during any crisis or chaos is the time, as we've told our Associates, to double down, not to retreat or freeze.

I can remember as far back as the 1990s, when I was a Realtor, I said to my wife, Kim, every time the market retreats, for whatever reason—and I'm not downplaying the virus right now; it's another market change. I said to her, "It's actually a great time if you're an entrepreneur, because the weak leave the market." Now, I'm not talking about just real estate. I'm talking about any niche or industry or business you're in. I don't care if you have a hot dog stand on the corner; you're going to lose competitors during this. It doesn't matter what business you're in. You have a choice to be the strong one, to double down versus retreat.

Now, again, let me share a personal example so you don't think this is just me blabbing away and throwing ideas at you here. My accountability partner, Stephen Woessner, who I'm very thankful to have as a part of the Wicked Smart Community and as a part of our life, has a chapter in this book. We didn't stop doing our calls because both of us were going through chaos. We doubled down. I mentioned my coach, Jairek. I didn't stop coaching. I renewed for another six months despite the cost. Zach and Nick and the entire Smart Real Estate Coach team and I didn't stop coaching because this happened. We doubled down and hired a coach who was teaching us how to do more virtually. We didn't stop hiring people because of this. We doubled down and added a brand manager, and we're looking for another part-time bookkeeper.

More times than ever, you can think through how this can benefit you versus how it's beaten you up. I know they're both there; we're all going through this together. Let me give you another example. Right now you can borrow from your 401(k) or your IRA, or someone you know who can, can help you. There's an idea for you. And as of the time of this chapter, to the best of my knowledge, that is a three-year payback, not a sixty-day payback. I'm just pointing out more positive that can and will come from chaotic times if you look and work at it.

Money from banks and from lines of credit has never ever been cheaper. If you can't access your 401(k) or IRA, or if you don't have one, or if you can't access your cheap credit lines or credit cards because you don't have credit, could you perhaps pull in a partner? Could you perhaps pull in someone who has an IRA or a 401(k), or who has good credit? Yes, you can. You can say to them, "Look, I know of a niche in real estate, and I know of a group, I know of a movement, the Smart Real Estate Coach community, the Wicked Smart Community, and they'll help me. They'll guide me. I want to jump on their island. Please help me financially, and I'll give you a percentage of my profits." That's just an idea. That's one idea on how to thrive. That's precisely what I did once in order to join a mastermind group I wanted and needed but couldn't afford.

The decisions you make in chaotic times can and will change things for you for the next decade. We don't want to be just good guys during times like this. We don't. We have a choice to be beyond that. It's a movement. It's a family. It's the Wicked Smart Community. It's outstanding.

Who do you want to become? Whether you're part of our community, or whether you're on an island by yourself, or whether you're on another island with another community that you love, it's okay. Who do you want to become this decade? The next few months will decide that.

*chapter 1*

# SMALL STEPS LEAD TO BIG SUCCESS

## *By Zachary Beach*

It was years of drug abuse, mediocrity, and personal doubt that led me to this night. I was twenty-one years old, and it was the night after Thanksgiving. I woke up from a dead sleep, I could hardly breathe, and the room was spinning. After I took a cold shower and worked through some breathing exercises, my heart began to slow down, and I finally caught my breath. I had suffered from another panic attack. That night was the last time I had to go through that awful feeling and the last time I used opioids.

I am sure you are wondering why I am telling my story about drug abuse and how this is related to success in real estate. It has everything to do with it.

Let me bring you back to the beginning that eventually led me to this point. I primarily grew up in a household with a single mother, as my dad was in and out of the picture for long periods of time. As you can imagine, that put a lot of pressure on my mom, but she always made ends meet, and she always did her best to get me everything I needed. I have two brothers, but they were much older than me, growing up and going off to college by the time I was in grade school. I was basically an only child growing up.

Because of this I had a lot of freedom and downtime. For the most part, I chose wisely and engaged in productive activities such as sports. I played a sport every season. Football was my favorite in the summer and fall, basketball in the winter, and baseball in the spring. When I wasn't playing sports, I found myself getting into trouble. I was a young boy with too much free time and not enough guidance. The friends I surrounded myself with were all in the same boat, so getting into trouble and not caring about school became the "cool" way to be. This led me to spend a large majority of my younger years in what most people would think is a state of mediocrity. Honestly, I think I was just bored with school. It didn't get me going.

Either way, I almost failed out of high school. To understand the extent, I had this ingenious plan to get out of class. I would get in trouble on Thursdays so that I was suspended for Friday and Monday—four-day weekend! That was what I would tell myself. The short-term ecstasy wore off once I realized I would have to spend the summer in class because I wouldn't meet the quota that state regulations established for hours spent in class. This lasted until about my junior year.

No wonder all my teachers thought I wouldn't be going to college. If it wasn't for my passion for football and a very special teacher who would constantly check on me, I would have failed out of school. Her name was Mrs. McSweeney. She was a calm woman, but I did my best to turn her into a fireball. She would go so far as chase me down the hallway and make sure I made it to class. She was my first mentor outside of my family, and she kept me from being another high school dropout in the Beach family. If she is reading this now, I would love to thank her for helping me through a tough time in my life.

College was a bit better. My first year was a huge success because I was coming off the high of having approval from my family for going to college. I don't think anyone thought that I was going to make it out of high school, let alone college. But I did!

The sense of mediocrity soon came rearing its head once again. Sophomore through senior year in college was filled with partying and some studying. I did just enough studying to get by. I managed to graduate, though.

Oh yes, and throughout this whole journey, I still had the little thing called a drug problem. It started when I was ten years old, when I smoked weed for the first time. I remember it clearly. I was hanging out in the unfinished basement of one of my friends. You know the ones that you have to enter through the bulkhead, and the walls and floors are cement. I was there with a small group of my friends, about five or six of us. One of my friends' older cousin was visiting from out of town. He joined us in the basement. He began smoking and asked if we would like to try it. I had been around older kids smoking marijuana many times, so I am not sure what made that day the day to try it. Maybe it was out of curiosity. I don't think it was peer pressure, as I have never been someone to do things just because other kids did it. But whatever the reason, I did it.

Also, when I was in fourth grade, I badly injured my knee playing football and needed surgery. Postsurgery, for my recovery, I was prescribed opioids to help relieve the pain. That was the first time I was introduced to prescription drugs. I am sure you are thinking that it's crazy to give a fourth grader prescription drugs, and I would have to agree with you. Since I was introduced to multiple drugs at such a young age, drug use and being around those who used drugs was the norm. As you can imagine, as I got older, things progressively got worse. It took years of off-and-on drug abuse before I realized I needed to make a change. I am grateful that I was paying attention to my actions and that I had an amazing girlfriend (my now wife, Kayla, Chris's daughter) and family who supported me and held up a mirror to all my blind spots. Unfortunately, I now get calls on a regular basis that my friends or acquaintances from high school have died from an overdose. It seems as if it is a common occurrence.

I tell you my demons in the hope that you find inspiration in my story and to bring context to the significant changes I had to make in order to avoid being another statistic. I don't believe in excuses. I believe strongly that there is always a path if you are looking for one. It was in those moments that I realized small steps can in fact lead to big successes.

Let's go back to that Thanksgiving night when I was twenty-one years old and had just suffered another panic attack. I was sleeping at my mother's house, so I crept halfway down the stairs and yelled to her, "Mom, I need to tell you something!" It was in the middle of the night, and my yell woke her up. In a daze she asked me what was wrong. I told her about my addiction and my panic attacks. She is an amazing woman and handled everything with tender care, as she knew how fragile I was at the time.

The next day I checked in to Adcare outpatient therapy. For the next ninety days, I attended three-hour-long meetings where twenty to thirty people and I discussed our problems and potential solutions and gave one another support. From day one, I knew that this place could give me a jump start, but it would not solve my problem. I was the only one who could solve my problem. My journey and passion for personal development began here. I began researching mentors by watching YouTube videos, reading books, and listening to books on CDs. What I discovered was that I had to make two major shifts if I was going to be successful:

1. change my mental state

2. change my physical state

I started with what I knew. I shifted my physical state. I grew up playing sports and spent a lot of time in the weight room. This was familiar to me, and I decided it was the easiest first small step to success. I joined a local CrossFit gym because an old trainer of mine had recently taken it over. His name is Coach Kyie. Kyie stands about five eleven and weighs about 220 pounds. He has the strength of an ox and the stamina of a deer. He knew my family well and understood the things I had gone through. He made it his personal mission to whip me into shape and to push me physically.

The most powerful thing he taught me was something he called "beast mode." Beast mode is being exhausted, mentally and physically. I felt I could no longer keep going, but I decided to reach down deep inside and find the strength to keep going. Once I had found that inner strength, I was able to go back to it again and again when things got tough. Eventually I began to accelerate at the hardest parts of a workout, and finishing strong became the norm. Although I do not train with him regularly now, I can still hear him yelling, "Beast mode!" at the top of his lungs when I am working out or when times are tough.

Training with him didn't just get me into peak condition. It was also a step to building my confidence. See, when you abuse your mind and body for so long, your confidence erodes and eventually disappears. I knew that if I was to be successful, I had to have confidence in myself. Each workout that I did and was successful at created a small building block for me to stand on. After about a year of training, I had a wall of confidence to stand on, which allowed me to take the next step in my life.

Now that my physical health was taken care of, it was time to turn my full attention on altering my state of mind. I started by searching YouTube for inspirational videos to listen to while I worked out. I enjoyed listening to Bob Proctor, Les Brown, and Tony Robbins, among others. At this point in my life, I didn't enjoy reading, but I did enjoy listening to powerful stories and motivational messages. Soon enough, I began to embrace reading books, which led me to *Think and Grow Rich*, by Napoleon Hill, and *The Science of Getting Rich*, by W. D. Wattles. As soon as I began reading these books, my mind began to expand, and my perspective began to change.

The biggest mental shift came when I began to use journaling in my daily routine. Taking time to get my thoughts, behaviors, actions, and emotions on paper helped me see who I truly was. It helped me analyze why I had certain thoughts, why I behaved in certain ways, and why I had a certain attitude in all areas of my life. This exercise brought clarity to my life. Now that I finally could think clearly, I could utilize the new knowledge I was learning and make huge shifts in my life. I now had clarity of my goals, my actions, my behaviors, and my attitude. This all allowed me to choose what knowledge I needed to acquire to move toward my goals. Lastly, I now had ways to motivate myself to take action on the knowledge I had acquired. I now had the mental foundation I had been looking for: clarity, knowledge, and motivation.

With my new physical and mental state as my support system, I eventually graduated from the University of Massachusetts Dartmouth with a degree in marketing. I could now check that box off the list. The problem was, I had never given much thought to what I wanted to do when I graduated. My original motivation for attending college was to prove all the people wrong who had doubted

I would amount to anything. I didn't give much thought to what I would do with the degree once I got it.

I was in a bit of limbo, so I went back to my mental building blocks. I realized that I needed to be clear on what I wanted to do next. I could not find clarity on what my career was going to be, but I did have clarity on one thing. I wanted to move to Newport, Rhode Island, and live near the water. I had been visiting Newport since I was in high school because my wife, Kayla (girlfriend at the time), and her family had a second home there. It was one of the most beautiful places I had ever been. Plus, I was passionate about not returning to central Massachusetts. Not because it was a bad place to live but because I felt I had outgrown the area and did not want to constantly be reminded of my past. Once I decided that, the best next step would be to start bartending full time to pay the bills. In college I needed a way to make money, so I began working at a local bar as a barback and bouncer. By the time I decided I was going to move permanently to Rhode Island, I had become a bartender. I was not ecstatic about the idea, but it helped me accomplish one of my goals.

Next I realized that in order for me to be happy and bring balance to my life, I needed to pursue my passion for health and fitness by becoming a personal trainer. I knew a lot about health and fitness, but I did not know the science behind the human body. There was a lot I had to learn—the name and function of each muscle group, the name and location of each bone, and the name and location of each tendon and ligament, just to name a few. This was quite a bit of knowledge that I would need to acquire, because to become a licensed personal trainer, you must pass a test. Balancing bartending four to five nights a week and studying for my test was a challenge. I needed to stay motivated.

I learned an exercise to use any time I needed motivation. I would write down a list of all the reasons why I wanted to be, do, or have something. This list would make it clear to me why I needed to give my full effort toward my passion. Originally, I needed external motivation. I needed someone on YouTube telling me a story of hardship or of triumph to get me moving. Now, I had developed the skill to find internal motivation. The difference is that external motivation only lasts during the moment, but internal motivation last forever because you can constantly go back to it every time you need a boost. I would revisit this list each day, especially when I was tired from a long night and didn't want to study or during moments when I wanted to give up. I have gone through multiple transitions in my life, and none of them were easy. But with each transition, I acquired new skills that allowed me to be successful more quickly.

I passed the test and became a personal trainer. It was my first taste of being an entrepreneur. I was in a new industry with zero clients. I had no idea where to start, so I reached out to a friend who is a personal trainer and asked how to get started. He invited me to speak with a local gym owner who also was a personal trainer. After a long conversation, he told me I could train at his gym. That was fantastic news and a small step that showed me that I was on the right track. The bad news was that now I had just added overhead to my cash flow, because I needed to pay the gym owner rent to train there. I needed to find clients and find them now.

The first place I could think of to look for them was at the bar. I had established a great reputation at the bar, and people trusted me. I told them that I was now personal training, so if they were looking to lose weight or stay fit for the summer, to let me know. My first client was a bartender I worked with. I was grateful for her, because it took another month before I began working with more clients.

It was a struggle at first to find clients, but then I began receiving referrals. On top of that, the timing was great as the season changed into summer. That meant everyone who had summer homes in the area would need a trainer for the summer.

Things were great for about two years. I was now a head bartender and had great shifts, and I was an established personal trainer and had consistent clients. My schedule looked like this most days:

4:30 a.m.: wake up
5:00 a.m.–10:00 a.m.: train clients
10 a.m.–11:00 a.m.: personal workout
12:00 p.m.–4:00 p.m.: sleep
5:00 p.m.–1:00 a.m.: bartend
2:00 a.m.–4:30 a.m.: sleep

Writing out my old schedule reminds me of how exhausted I was. I did this five days a week, and the only days I had completely off were Sundays. By the time I was twenty-four years old, I was beginning to plot my next move. I was burning the candle at both ends and knew this could not last forever. My wife, Kayla, was working just as hard as I was, and I knew we had to make a change. Not only was the schedule beating us up mentally and physically, but we had hopes and dreams to have a family one day. That could not happen in our current circumstances.

You may be familiar with this part of my story, but at age twenty-five, I reached out to my father-in-law, Chris, to discuss the potential of Kayla and me working with him and Nick (my brother-in-law) in real estate. I honestly had no idea if I was going to like it or be successful in it, but I knew that I needed a change. I began dipping my toe in the water by making outbound calls during my afternoon breaks instead of sleeping. I did this for four months before I went full time. Kayla made the transition first and joined the family team in March 2016, and I joined the family team in April 2016. We completely burned the bridges. Kayla and I both stopped bartending, and I stopped personal training.

You may be thinking, "That is crazy! Why wouldn't you keep your foot in the door and still train or still bartend?" The best thing for me was to focus on one goal and commit my full self to it. I had decided at that time that I was going to be a successful real estate investor, and I knew that bartending and personal training would suck the energy out of me and distract me from my goal. Having clarity of my goal forced me to do everything in my power to acquire the knowledge of the business and lit a fire under my butt. No better motivation than starting from zero.

The transition to be a real estate investor had its ups and downs. I had zero experience, so every single piece of the business was new to me. I had to learn everything from scratch. Luckily, I had guidance from my new teammates and, most importantly, my father-in-law. My first position in the company consisted of the basic duties we now delegate to a virtual assistant. My job was to make outbound calls, lots of outbound calls, to sellers whose contract with a Realtor had recently expired. I had a basic script, a document with answers to sellers' commonly asked questions, and a document we call the property-information lead sheet, which consisted of questions that we needed answered to determine if the property was a good fit for us to purchase.

At the time, we had no formal training in place. My training consisted of making phone calls, stumbling over my words, and then asking Chris or Nick their opinion on how I could have handled the call better. I spent hours and hours on the phone deliberately practicing my scripts. I would send all my calls to Chris to critique, and some of those were painful.

At first I was awful, but over time I naturally began getting more and more comfortable. This meant I could now be in the moment and think and respond to a seller in a natural conversation. That was my first breakthrough and reassurance that I had made the correct decision to get involved in real estate. I don't recall the exact moment, but it was around the ninety-day mark. At first it was a struggle to acquire leads, but as my confidence continued to grow, leads became easier and easier to acquire.

The next step in my progression was to begin taking calls to the next level. Up until this time, I would simply gather information, and Chris would make the next call. Getting to the next level for me meant getting past surface-level motivation and discovering how we could truly help solve a seller's problem. This also meant walking a seller through our process and painting a picture of the seller's new future with their problem solved. I was taking more control and managing the leads through our process.

As the months progressed, I began taking over more and more of the responsibility of the front end of the business. At roughly 180 days in, I was going on almost all appointments. I can remember my first appointment like it was yesterday. It was an old 1800s house in central Massachusetts. The seller was a schoolteacher, and he had recently been divorced. He was looking for closure and just wanted to be done with it. Not only was that the first appointment I went on without the support of my team, but it became the first property that I would purchase. From then on, I would play a very strong role in the entire front end of our business. I became what we now call a Seller Specialist.

I still had not mastered the business, and I humbly say that even now I learn something new on a weekly or monthly basis. For the next six months, I dedicated myself to learning everything I could about structuring deals, negotiating, building rapport, and dealing with the legalities in our business. The learning never ends, and that's one of the many ways our Associates benefit from locking arms with us and working together.

After a year in the business, I felt very confident in my skills to acquire and close deals with sellers. It was time to begin understanding the rest of the business. After multiple position shifts in the company, Nick found his place as the Buyer Specialist. He would handle everything once we had a property under contract as far as getting it sold, which included marketing and dealing with all the buyer calls and prequalifying.

I began spending more time looking over his shoulder, helping him make buyer calls and run buyer meetings, and sitting in on attorney signings. I wanted to master the business, and it was important to me that I understood all sides of it.

It took me about a year to be comfortable handling all aspects of the buyer side. I am a firm believer that we all have our strengths and weaknesses and that we should focus on our strengths. Nick is a master at understanding buyers, bringing them through the process, increasing their deposits, and getting them to the finish line. I had no desire to switch my role, but I am an entrepreneur at heart, and I have to be able to run all aspects of the business, know the processes, and be able to execute if I am ever called on. Nick also works hand in hand with the Associates, of course, and with all their buyers, which is invaluable, because that's where the 3 Paydays are created!

Once I was comfortable with buying and selling properties, it was time to understand how to manage those properties. When I say "manage," it is not in the sense of a landlord or a property manager but as a cash flow manager. As our portfolio of properties increased, the importance of having systems and processes in place to collect Paydays #1 and Paydays #2 and deposit our monthly payments to the mortgage lender, bank, or seller became essential. At this point, Chris and Kayla were running this part of the business. I spent the next year making sure I had an in-depth understanding of it. This was the first time I had been introduced to financial statements. Profit and loss statements alone took me a good deal of time to understand. This was the part of the business that took the most time to click, but once it did, it opened my eyes to all the possibilities of the business.

It took me three years to understand the business in its entirety—which is ironic in that we ask every Associate that we accept to commit to working this business for three years. It has taken me almost ten years of self-improvement and discovery to understand how I am able to take on new ventures with zero experience and find success.

**Step 1**: Find clarity.

**Step 2**: Acquire knowledge with mentors and coaches—success leaves clues.

**Step 3**: Use internal and external motivation to create momentum.

My journey has had many ups and downs, and I am sure you have experienced the same. The need to draw attention to both your mental and physical states if you want to make a change is critical to your success. I suggest spending a great deal of time working on your mindset, reflecting and bringing clarity to your world. I also suggest spending time improving your health and physical body, as I have found that my confidence and belief in myself grows when I feel good. Use the three-step system above to create change in your life or when you are in a state of transition.

I encourage you to take one of these learning lessons and implement it immediately rather than trying to take on all at once.

Then revisit this chapter and implement the next. Small steps lead to big successes.

I'd love to have a strategy call with you and help guide you further.

# chapter 2

# ON YOUR TERMS—
# WHAT THAT MEANS

My son, Nick, was thirteen years old when a snowboarding accident left him in a coma with doctors telling us he'd never walk, talk, or eat on his own again.

Nick, a good student with an outgoing personality and close relationships with everyone in the family, was with his school ski club on Mount Wachusett in Princeton, Massachusetts, when the accident happened on February 5, 2003. I got a cell phone call in my car from the school—one no parent wants to receive. The woman on the other end said, "Your son has had an accident, and it is too windy to life flight 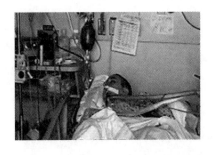 him, so he's headed to the hospital in an ambulance." I headed to UMass Memorial Medical Center. As I drove, reality hit me: *My son could be crippled or die.* If you have children and have never said that to yourself, you are lucky. My chest felt like it was caving in; my eyes welled up, which scared me even more, because I rarely cry. I frantically tried to leave messages for my wife to meet me at the hospital. When

Kim arrived, we didn't have words—we just embraced. Shortly after Kim arrived, the emergency room staff came out with a bag of Nick's clothes and boots, which had to be cut from his body.

We would learn later that it had been icy that day on the slopes. Nick, an accomplished athlete and experienced, aggressive snowboarder, went off a twenty-five-foot jump and at the very top caught an edge with his snowboard. He had forgotten his helmet that day, and when he hit the ground, he tumbled, causing multiple brain injuries. He was spared more severe brain damage—or possible death—only because of the presence of one of only three or four paramedics in all of New England qualified to perform an intubation, the delicate procedure of putting a tube down his throat for oxygen to flow.

More than six hours after I received that first phone call, we finally were allowed to see Nick. No other moment in my life has been that shocking and intense. We entered a room lighted only by the more than ten machines hooked up to him. He was a shadow on the bed—a lump, not moving. I was scared and felt powerless. As the doctor explained each machine and what organ it supported, our minds swirled. He was in a coma. His head on one side was swollen like a basketball, and he had purple and black bruises all over his face and head.

Doctors came in to speak to us for the first of many consultations and decisions about Nick's life that would become a normal part of our day for the next eighty-five days. Our first decision: because of the pressure in Nick's head, the surgeon needed permission to drill a burr hole in his skull for a catheter to relieve the pressure.

Doctors said to start planning weeks instead of days for our stay at the hospital.

As the weeks went by, each tube that came out, each machine that turned off, every monitor that switched off was a huge deal. A major milestone came when we wheeled Nick into Franciscan

Hospital for Children and his rehabilitation journey began. The second week there, he was able to sit up with support from nurses for two minutes—another major accomplishment.

We started to fill the walls in Nick's room with affirmations. He still could not speak and had barely enough strength to communicate using hand signs, but he read the signs on his walls. Nick doesn't remember anything from the weeks he was in a coma but says his family's optimism and positive energy made a difference in his remarkable recovery. "One day I was in a wheelchair at Franciscan, and I said to my mom, 'Am I going to ever be able to walk again?' and she said, 'Of course you are.' It's right then I realized that I would be okay," Nick recalled later.

He exhausted himself performing twelve hours a day of physical, occupational, and speech therapy. At night, when he was supposed to be resting, I would walk past his room and see him working with weights. Kim and I asked his doctors and therapists to all get together and meet with us to do game planning, something they had never done before for a patient.

"Nick was very much focused," recalled Kim Pinch, one of the physical therapists. "He was always joking, always cooperative—but he had a very specific task in mind." Nick made goals for himself: to be able to eat a grinder, drink a Coke, and finally jog out of the hospital.

> *Realizing that life events can happen at any time has informed my business decision-making and inspired my desire to help others.*

Nick did just that—and it was a lesson in setting clear goals and using clear steps, family support, and game plans to reach those goals. Realizing that life events can happen at any time has informed my business decision-making and inspired my desire to help others.

Thinking back about a time when we accomplished the impossible by having the family work together as a team has been a lesson I could apply, and not just in the comeback from the 2008 debacle. Deals can go awry, as you will read in chapter 10. But just as my family came together for Nick, my family business comes together to help our clients by having clearly defined goals and the steps to reach them.

There were people who told Nick and us that he couldn't expect to walk again, people who didn't want to participate in the goal-setting meetings we asked for. But we set up our own terms and our plan to fulfill his goal of literally running out of the hospital. He also caught up with his class, graduated from high school on time, and became a real estate agent and motivational speaker.

Personal tragedy can hit at any time. Too many people think they can't find a way—as we did—to care for a sick child or elderly parent. They say, "I'm torn. I should be there, but I've got to run my business." It's awful. But if you set your business up properly on YOUR TERMS, it can and will run on its own.

This was the case when my father had a heart scare on Fourth of July weekend in 2015, and I left for Maine with a two-hour notice to spend some time with my brother and him there. It was also the case when Kim's dad had Alzheimer's before he passed away in the spring of 2016, and we made the drive to Massachusetts from Rhode Island probably three days a week. We wanted to, and we were able to do that. When my brother passed away in 2010 at the young age of forty-seven, we were able to be with family each and every day we chose to.

As for Nick, after living in a ten-by-ten-foot hospital room for many months, he wanted to skip college and go into real estate after high school. I said, "Okay. If you're up for a strict curriculum, we'll put one together." With training from many of my mentors and friends, we structured courses, seminars, trips, and things that he could go to and learn. That became his hands-on curriculum for the next several years. He joined my investment business full time in fall of 2014 after six years as a successful licensed real estate agent and now plays a pivotal role in both the property side of our companies and the coaching side.

**RENT-TO-OWN:**

A lease or rental contract that includes the option to purchase a home for a set price (with a down payment or deposit), monthly payments for a period of time, and then a payment of the balance of the purchase price. In this book, rent-to-own and lease-purchase are used synonymously.

Today, among other roles, Nick helps the buyers through the entire process from the phone call to sitting down and signing on their **rent-to-own** home or other terms. Nick has continually fine-tuned his area as a buyer specialist and has helped us almost double our per-deal profits from down payments.

He also assists Associates all over North America with their properties doing the same thing as we do.

*Nick before the accident, third from the right in the back row.*

*Nick before the accident.*

*Nick after the accident, with his speech therapist at Franciscan.*

*Nick after the accident, when he was able to return home.*

*Nick after the accident, at a Franciscan event with Tim Wakefield.*

## THE TEAM BEHIND BUYING AND SELLING ON YOUR TERMS

Kim and I have a family business that focuses on helping people reach their goal of home ownership, which many thought they could never achieve. Our daughter, Kayla, used to be the general manager for our real estate and coaching companies and now is the best mom on the planet, caring for two wonderful children, Remi and Bellamy. She still works very closely with me on one of our out-of-state properties and oversees some higher-level things at Smart Real Estate Coach. Her husband, Zach Beach, works on generating leads, acquiring properties, and buying in our property entities while working with our coaching clients and Associates. He has been with us since December 2015 and has grown into a COO (chief operating officer) role with Smart Real Estate Coach.

While we are helping coaching clients and Associates with their income goals and real estate businesses, the family business also helps other buyers and sellers who, for various reasons, are in the real estate market. We get some buyers who are in financial trouble, while others have no financial challenges at all but still want to utilize our purchasing methods for various reasons; some of those include just time to save more of a down payment, time to show "seasoning" to the lender. On the seller side, we are dealing with people who perhaps can't get the price they need or want for their home. Maybe they owe as much as or more than it's worth, and a short sale would damage their credit. Or they may be builders or rehabbers who want to avoid the expense of a real estate agent fee or have accounting and tax reasons to not sell right away but want to get their maximum cash-out in a longer-term deal. We have many sellers who are retiring and don't need to sell but are tired of running properties they own.

On the buyer side, we have two main categories: people who have credit challenges and the self-employed. The credit challenges have always been there, but banks have raised requirements. I don't see banks making things easier in the future, which simply strengthens our model more and more. The self-employed used to be able to walk into a bank and get a **stated-income loan**. They have cash for a down payment, but while their accountant may have helped them structure their business in a tax-smart way, the bank now demands they report their income to the IRS differently for two years (this changes from time to time with banks and mortgage companies) before they can get a mortgage. Their credit needs "seasoning"—but if they find us, they can get into a home in the meantime and lock in a price.

In chapter 6, you will read about all the different ways we can structure a profitable deal while helping both the buyer and the seller. We describe **Six Buckets,** which are different ways we can make a deal with sellers to take control of their property and get it

**SIX BUCKETS:**

The different options a seller can fall into:
1. Assign Out (AO)
2. Sandwich lease
3. Owner financing
4. Subject To (ST)
5. Wholesale
6. Optioning

sold. For almost every seller who calls us, one or another of the buckets is a good option. Making a smart choice of bucket requires data and experience, and that's where coaching comes in. You can start with no experience if you are coachable, have the discipline, and invest the time.

A coach also can teach you to recognize a true prospect versus a complete time waster. For example, sellers who want over retail value or want all the monthly income they can get out of their property with no willingness to share it with you don't really want to work out something on YOUR TERMS. We can save hours of time and a lot of headaches by using automation and systems to screen out people who really just want a conventional sale.

When I first started making these deals, I hired a coach who spent a good six months in the trenches with me. Each time I thought a deal was structured, I'd call immediately and say, "Is this right? Let me send you everything." Within sixty days we had our first deal done, but it was six or seven months before I felt like I had mastered the process enough to forgo that phone call.

## NINE STEPS TO SUCCESS:

1. Locating seller prospects
2. Prequalifying seller prospects
3. Using follow-up properly and efficiently
4. Placing the seller in the proper bucket
5. Structuring and presenting offers
6. Following up on offers
7. Signing or closing
8. Locating buyer prospects
9. Getting the property sold

In real estate we're always learning. We have to make adjustments in some deals. There can be expensive lessons if you're not careful, but you shorten the learning curve by leaning on somebody who's already done it. I've spent more than $300,000 on training so you don't have to.

When I make reference to coaching or coaches versus mentoring, I do that for a reason. To me, a mentor is more of a consultant or adviser only, whereas a coach rolls up their sleeves and runs alongside you. In our case, we coach our Associates by working in their business with them to set things up properly, speak with sellers, speak with buyers, structure deals, and so much more.

In chapter 4, you will see that there is a logical, systematic way to make deals on YOUR TERMS: the **Nine Steps to Success**. The first steps are essential for any business, but each one is quite a learning step. We refer to someone who has mastered the Nine Steps to Success and is ready to do these deals as a transaction engineer.

I think of an engineer as someone who figures problems out and comes to a logical win-win solution. A transaction engineer is able to look at a property-information sheet, debrief a seller, structure the right deal, and then place it in the right bucket.

### The Mentors and Coaches

Each and every year I personally pick what seminars, mastermind groups, mentors, and/or coaches I think I should utilize in order to make it the best year ever. Our team does the same thing, and then we each pick what we call a specialized training for ourselves that doesn't involve the team.

### The Buyer Specialist

**Nick Prefontaine** grew up in the real estate industry, swinging a hammer and doing cleanups at condo conversions at age sixteen, and knocking on preforeclosure doors at seventeen, just a few years after his miraculous rehabilitation from multiple brain injuries. Franciscan Hospital for Children presented him with the prestigious Profile in Courage Award in 2005. Nick now specializes in working with our buyers who are entering into rent-to-own agreements or owner-financing agreements with us, while also helping our coaching clients and Associates. He has spoken to rapt audiences at high schools, awards ceremonies, corporate regional conferences, business associations, medical center openings, fundraising events, and our own annual events.

### The Managers

Executive assistant and head of business development: **Kristen Gallant**; marketing director: **Lauren Bulk**; and **Susan Skipper**, who runs the properties with Nick and Zach.

My daughter, **Kayla,** used to be general manager, and now she is an amazing wife and mom, raising her amazing kids, Remi and Bellamy. She continues to help me as she oversees all operations as well as some distant out-of-state properties.

**Ryan Staples** is the director of creative media at Smart Real Estate Coach. He handles many areas of digital branding and in-house marketing, including video production, graphic design, and web development. He began designing websites when he was ten years old. Not long after that, he got his hands on a camcorder and started playing with analog video  editing, casting his younger brother and sister to act in sketches and short films that he wrote. In 2011, Ryan got an account management job at a business consulting firm, eventually working his way up to the position of creative director. He prides himself on the personal touch that he brings to media production work, ensuring that it's coated with a professional sheen but never looks automated or overly produced. Ryan is a passionate fan of Boston sports. In his free time, he enjoys reading, art, film, and writing as a creative outlet—be it short stories, novels, films, or television scripts. He's also been performing stand-up comedy since 2010, working all the major clubs and casinos in the area. Ryan lives in Worcester, Massachusetts, with his wife and son.

**Colleen Murphy** was born and raised in Newport, Rhode Island. She attended Providence College and graduated from American International College. Colleen is the mother of two wonderful children.

She is the business manager at Chew Publishing, Inc. and in her free time enjoys spending time with her family at the beach.

### The COO, Partner, and Coach

**Zachary Beach** has become part owner of Smart Real Estate Coach and currently serves as COO and coach to the higher-level Associates alongside me. He also runs Pre Property Solutions with Nick Prefontaine. Zachary majored in marketing and minored in finance at UMass Dartmouth and continues to sharpen his skills to help grow the company while coaching and educating our Wicked Smart Community.

### The Life Partner

My wife for more than thirty-four years (as of August 2020), **Kim Prefontaine** has worked with me in every capacity throughout my career. Kim and I met when we were twelve years old in middle school English class. She is an amazing judge of character. Her real estate specialty is construction projects, whether building from the ground up or rehabbing, such as condo conversions or fixing and flipping houses. She is also an amazing interior designer. Her raise-the-roof projects, such as putting a second floor on a ranch home, earned a write-up in the *Boston Globe*. She continues to work with all of us, always bringing new and refreshing insights and ideas to the table.

*chapter 3*

# YEAH, BUT (FILL IN YOUR SELF-IMPOSED ROADBLOCK HERE)

So you think doing a deal on YOUR TERMS is starting to sound great, but you don't understand how it works.

I'll start with a simple example. After forming my company, Pre Property Solutions, our first terms deal was in Middletown, Rhode Island. I did a direct-mail solicitation, known in the industry as a yellow letter because it appears to be hand-written on yellow paper. It arrives in an invitation-style envelope and is appealing and sparks curiosity, so it gets opened. This mailing went to people who owned a home outright with no mortgage. The owner of a three-bedroom ranch home responded. The value was roughly $235,000, according to my **appraisal**, and the seller wanted a minimum of $220,000 because he factored in what he might

**APPRAISAL:**

The process of putting a value on property, including land and buildings. Appraisals of real estate may happen for various reasons and arrive at different types of values. A bank writing a mortgage may place a market value on a property that differs from the eventual sale price because buyers are willing to pay more or less for that property.

have received after an offer and after paying a Realtor. Everything seemed fine there.

### ASSIGN/ASSIGNMENT:

When ownership of a mortgage or other real estate asset is transferred from one company or individual to another, it is called an assignment. We have a legal equitable interest; first we procure the buyer, then we assign that buyer and related contract back to the seller.

The seller agreed to a lease-purchase and wanted $1,500 a month. We were going to procure the tenant-buyer and then **assign** the buyer back to the seller to handle. (This type of deal and other options will be explained later in the book and was referred to earlier as an Assign Out, or AO.) The home had been on the market with a local real estate agent for ten months with no success, but in just eleven days, through our signs and our marketing, we procured a very strong tenant-buyer and sold him the property for $235,000. The buyer had been driving by the original For Sale sign almost daily for those ten months but called us when he saw our sign because it specifically said "Lease/Purchase NO BANKS." The big difference there? *Terms.*

We got a nonrefundable down payment of $23,500, which we split with the seller, and beat the seller's monthly target of $1,500 by getting the buyer to pay $1,680 (we always try to start slightly over the seller's minimum goal even though the profit monthly—Payday #2—is all retained by the seller). Our half of the down payment, $11,750, satisfied us at the time as an adequate fee for assigning the rights to our buyer back to our seller, although we have since learned that we can keep three-quarters or all of the down payment as long as the seller achieves their goal of net cash.

The seller netted $223,250—more than he expected—pocketed $1,680 a month for twenty-four months, and kept the title until getting the balance prior to the end of the term. On or before the end of the term, the buyer and seller have a closing on the property that is a standard closing. The vehicle that allowed this to happen was our lease-purchase with the seller, our procuring a tenant-buyer on a rent-to-own, and then our assigning the tenant-buyer back to the seller until such time as they are mortgage ready (financeable) and can obtain conventional financing to purchase. The buyer had two years to fix his credit and get a mortgage to pay that balance. It was very successful for the seller and simple for us, since the buyer became the seller's responsibility once we made the assignment. Getting half the down payment produced a nice paycheck for us, but you'll see that in the majority of our deals at Pre Property Solutions, we stay in and collect 3 Paydays.

A more complex deal involved a two-unit property in Webster, Massachusetts. The source was something I did personally at the time—called a FSBO (pronounced "fizz-bo" and meaning someone listing a home for sale by owner). The gentleman used to live in the home and was renting it out. He had the tenant from hell, who not only beat up his property but also stole his identity and ran up his credit cards. To say the least, this homeowner was fed up and didn't want anything more to do with the property or ever being a landlord again. That is the kind of challenge that we can help solve and be paid well for.

The mortgage balance was $169,000, and the property was worth $225,000. The seller, who was an accountant and particular with his numbers, agreed to a lease-purchase. We became the lease-purchaser of his property for the balance of his mortgage, meaning we would take over the monthly payments of $1,250. Our contracts allow us to not have to start that until such time as we procure our tenant-buyer in order to cover it. Once we had several properties under contract, several Paydays #1, #2, and #3 happening, and cash flow coming in, we had the flexibility to take some of those on by choice prior to finding a buyer (if the equity and upside was large enough, of course). We wrote a term of seventy-two months to give the mortgage principal time to be paid down. We then found a tenant-buyer who would be able to get a mortgage, but only after some **credit enhancement**. We sold the property for $225,000 with a $1,950 monthly payment to us, so we were clearing $700 monthly over the current

**CREDIT ENHANCEMENT:**

A process in which borrowers try to improve the reports that mortgage lenders receive about their creditworthiness. Borrowers can repair blemishes on their credit reports by correcting errors and systematically repaying debts.

mortgage payment. And we got a $15,000 nonrefundable down payment. The two-unit building suited a family that had the husband and wife living upstairs with their baby, and mom, dad, and grandmother living in the downstairs apartment. The area was not the greatest, but it was a fenced-in lot with an additional detached garage and a perfect fit for this family. I mentioned that this buyer needed credit enhancement, but sometimes we'll work with a buyer who happens to be self-employed and already has great credit but just needs time to show the bank or mortgage company proper income reporting. Other times someone will be in need of time to qualify because of a past foreclosure or bankruptcy. More on these other buyers later.

---

## PURCHASE TYPE:
### SANDWICH LEASE-PURCHASE

**TERM:** 72 MONTHS

**PURCHASE PRICE:** $169,000
(SELLER'S MORTGAGE BALANCE)

**SOLD:** $225,000 WITH $15,000 DOWN
AND $1,950/MONTH

**PAYDAY #1:** <u>$15,000</u> NONREFUNDABLE DOWN PAYMENT

**PAYDAY #2:** MONTHLY SPREAD OF $1,950 – $1,250 =
$700 x 72 MONTHS TOTALS <u>$50,400</u>

**PAYDAY #3:** $225,000 LESS $15,000 DOWN LESS
$135,000 MORTGAGE BALANCE AFTER SIX YEARS OF
PRINCIPAL PAYMENTS = <u>$75,000</u>

### TOTAL PAYDAYS: $140,400

---

This example shows the 3 Paydays: Payday #1, a deposit up front; Payday #2, a monthly spread, which is the difference between our buyer's payment in and our mortgage payment out; and Payday #3, the back-end/finance cash-out. Even after seeing how this type of deal has worked for us, our **coaching clients** sometimes doubt whether it will work for them. "Yeah, but ..." they say; their market is different, sellers in their area are different, or they have

### COACHING CLIENTS:

Our website, SmartRealEstateCoach.com, has a members-only area, ranging from online video lessons to personal coaching, consulting, and Joint-Venture Partnership programs. See the website's Products pages for details of the levels of membership and current pricing.

some other self-imposed roadblock keeping them from realizing their 3 Paydays.

Let's go over those "Yeah, but …" concerns one at a time.

**"Yeah, but,"** you say, "didn't you risk your family's own money by taking on the mortgage?"

Actually, not much at all, because I only put down a $10 deposit and spent $125 on a title search when I signed my lease-purchase agreement, and our taking over the mortgage payment was contingent upon me finding my buyer first. Only then did we start making the mortgage payments. We always had a sure bet. The mortgage stayed in the seller's name until cashed out.

**"Yeah, but,"** you say, "sounds great … so why aren't more people doing this?"

Why wasn't I doing it during my first twenty or so years in real estate? Because this type of deal is not conventional. It's been done for decades, yet sellers and buyers regularly say to me, "I've never heard of this. Is this new? Why aren't more people doing it? This sounds too good to be true." To take advantage of it, you only need to ask, "Why *not* me?" and come to believe that you actually can do it. And you have to learn how. The best way to learn is to grab on to the shirttail of someone (like me) who is doing it and allow him or her to teach you. Unfortunately, some of the people teaching this type of deal just sell the idea or the courses without the deeper knowledge and experience that comes from actually doing deals in the field. I have a very simple but effective recipe for any entrepreneur looking to achieve great things in any industry—not just real estate. Here it is:

1. Find an industry or niche area you can get excited about. In real estate, is it buying and selling on TERMS? Is it

wholesaling (more of a job)? Is it rehabbing (job!)? Is it apartments? What is it that you can wrap your arms around and get excited about? The TERMS business allows you to not utilize banks, not sign personally, not use large amounts of cash, and not chase and beg investors to put up money. Yeah, I'm a bit biased, but I'm not so naive as to think everyone will love what we do—so pick a niche. With access to the internet these days, you can do a lot of free research. Take us, for example. You can find us on YouTube, Facebook, our free webinar, our monthly free Wicked Smart Sit Downs on Zoom, and a whole bunch more.

> *The TERMS business allows you to not utilize banks, not sign personally, not use large amounts of cash, and not chase and beg investors to put up money.*

2. Within that niche, find someone you can relate to, someone you can trust (for example, if you were to choose our team to work with, we have five core values that we run by, and we're very blunt and to the point and all about doing deals), someone who is still actively working the niche you want to participate in (much too dangerous to follow someone who used to do deals and isn't active any longer—real estate changes rapidly, and you want to be with someone who has a finger on the pulse), and then, lastly, someone who is where you want to be (some have a great business but a crappy marriage, a great business but no lifestyle, a great business but a jerky personality ... you get the point).

3.  Now, this third step can be the toughest. After 1 and 2, it's time to buckle down. It's time to laser focus on crushing it in the niche you chose, and to do that, I suggest you manage your expectations as far as having success. When I say "manage expectations," I'm talking about not falling for the late-night TV commercials and online ads touting overnight success and becoming an overnight millionaire. That's a bunch of baloney. Real estate is a route to getting rich over time and attaining long-term rock-solid wealth— NOT to getting rich this month. In order to properly do this, it's time to put the blinders on and be coachable for thirty-six months. "Put the blinders on" means no looking back, no looking left or right—laser focused. You do this literally in any industry or niche, and after thirty-six months you will have had, in my opinion, an absolute breakthrough transformative experience.

Regardless of what stage of my businesses I was at over the past twenty-nine-plus years, I always found people doing what I wanted to do and learned from them.

> Regardless of what stage of my businesses I was at over the past twenty-nine-plus years, I always found people doing what I wanted to do and learned from them.

The learning curve is an important consideration. I ask people, "How old are you?" Let's say someone is thirty-five years old. My advice is, "Well, it took you thirty-five years to get here (and most aren't happy with 'here'), so be patient." If that person is a doctor, he or she will have spent the better part of nine years in college but may be making $150,000 or $200,000. If that person is a judge, he or she may have spent upward of eight years in college and many more years practicing law to be making $100,000.

Whatever the profession—teacher, architect, CPA—nothing else out there that I'm aware of, including franchises, can provide so much return for the time invested in learning and practicing as being a transaction engineer on YOUR TERMS. More on patience and timing will be found in chapter 11.

**"Yeah, but,"** you say, "don't you need special credentials or licensing?" Having been a real estate agent and having owned a real estate brokerage, I understand there are different perspectives on this question, and it is very important to disclose one's credentials and role. Anyone can become a transaction engineer and do deals on YOUR TERMS if you are willing to take the time to develop the skill sets necessary (the transaction engineer's Nine Steps to Success will be detailed in the next chapter). You can't skip steps or think you can just push a button or buy a magic product and have instant success. *Generally* speaking, if you have an equitable interest in a property or own a property, you are acting on your own behalf and are not conducting a service for others for a fee, and as such, you do not need a license. When was the last time you saw a FSBO (for sale by owner) get licensed to sell their own home?

Some states *do* require a license to assign an option. As of this writing, Illinois just passed a law that hurt a lot of wholesalers (not our niche; more of a job!), so we see a lot of them seeking out our niche of buying and selling on TERMS. With the advice of a local attorney, you can adapt YOUR TERMS, or you can add a real estate agent to your team. In Florida, a person who is not a principal in the company needs a license. For example, if you hire an acquisitionist on your team—like Zach is for us—he or she needs a license. The owner does not. Now, these are just two examples, and of course laws change constantly, so this is not legal or licensing advice of any type. We have Associates right now all over North America, and to my knowledge, there may be a tiny handful of those who are licensed because they already were when they started with us. Nothing against the continuing education that I had with the Realtors for years and years, but frankly it has nothing to do with what goes on in the field—just a side note.

I can tell you that my son, Nick, and I both resigned our real estate licenses when we got into buying and selling on OUR TERMS. There are two sides to this question on licensing. For me, I just didn't want to deal with the drama of having real estate agents calling me to scream and whine that I was trying to "steal" their listing because their client received some of our marketing materials or phone calls, which go out to general geographic areas. Since I am not a licensed real estate agent any longer, I don't get those calls. There's a disclosure on my website written by my attorney that says the following:

> *Prefontaine Properties and affiliated or subsidiary companies are not real estate brokers or agents. Prefontaine Properties is a real estate investment company. Prefontaine Properties is not a real estate brokerage and does not provide Realtor services to the public, or to any of the parties to which it has contractual relationships.*

My website disclosure goes on to say that if you are selling a home, we can purchase it, any price, condition, or area. We also can pay cash and close in five days from clear title, or we can structure a lease-purchase with you. That is a legal disclosure that my attorneys wrote to be very clear to the public that we are not providing a service. We are purchasing property and/or controlling it, and then offering it out to the public. Check with your attorney for appropriate disclosure guidelines for your area. Several years ago, one of the states we operate in had the licensing authority call me to say they thought I was acting as a Realtor. I explained my experience and what we were actually doing, and sent all our forms in to them. They responded with an unequivocal, "Okay, you're right. You are an investor, not performing a service." Done. Now, I'll tell you that it's highly likely they called because some wacko Realtors from my areas saw me buy up property they couldn't sell and called to whine. Just an inclination.

Also, if you're not going to go out and practice as a real estate agent and just want to be an investor, why waste a lot of hours and fees to keep up with the barely relevant continuing education required to keep a real estate license? And if you are a real estate agent in a company owned by someone else, that broker-owner will rightfully be entitled to a piece of your deal profits unless you have your own LLC or entity and have cleared that with your broker-owner. In my opinion you have the right to run any business you want for your family outside of your licensing-related work or duties with your office. I'm happy to discuss it with you on a private strategy call.

Readers already licensed may not want to give up their real estate license if their goal is just to add income streams. For example, they could note on a listing, "We have terms. We have owner financing." There are very few such listings. A real estate agent who becomes known as the terms expert can help almost any buyer or seller and can get some commissions through referrals from real estate agents who don't have another solution for some of their buyers and sellers. On the flip side, a terms expert may be working with a seller who, for whatever reason, decides to do a conventional sale, and the investor who is a licensed agent can pick up that commission. There are differing opinions on this subject among my mentors and various investor friends, so you will need to decide for yourself.

Our approach is to refer conventional sellers to real estate agents, who can't legally pay us for that referral but do share comparative market analysis information and refer business back to us. We no longer need a real estate agent to give us access to expired listings on the multiple listing service, because anyone can see a flood of these now by using one of the available services we have on our website under Resources. Prior to those being available, I simply paid a few hundred dollars monthly to have an assistant to a Realtor I know provide those to us.

One other advantage of having a real estate license is that, as a service covered by your license, you can assign a lease-purchase back to the seller—like in the deal at the beginning of this chapter— without first doing your own lease-purchase contract. Do I wish I had known how to buy and sell on terms all the years I was active as a Realtor? I sure do. I could have brought my homes sold from 100 up to 125 or more yearly, I'm sure. But clearly, I think the disadvantages of having a license outweigh the advantages.

**"Yeah, but,"** you say, "I don't have the money to get started."

Remember, I started this when I was just coming back from the downturn and had little to no capital. I was restructuring my business and couldn't spend money hiring someone to call prospective sellers.

I went through expired home-sale listings and FSBO ads and made calls myself, using scripts. I started off very slowly, with a few hours a few mornings a week. Only after the first deal described at the beginning of this chapter brought in an $11,750 down payment did I start to invest cash back into the business to ultimately grow it to where it is today, with our kids involved.

Think about the average deal proceeds mentioned in this book's prologue—Payday #2—$409 monthly (for twenty-four to forty-eight months!); Payday #1—about $28,000 up front; and Payday #3—about $30,000 on the back end. Just one of those deals is enough to fund an assistant to do calls and begin to very slowly, very carefully, very conservatively scale your business. What if you just did one to six deals a year and provided those nice Paydays for yourself and your family?

**"Yeah, but,"** you say, "I can't believe it's possible to start with no money." Of course you need to spend a few hundred dollars at the beginning or maybe a few thousand dollars spread over time. A virtual phone system, which provides small businesses with professional call answering and forwarding, may cost $25 or $45 a month. If you can't design a website yourself, you may end up paying someone to do so, but we have a web designer who can build a done-for-you site just like ours. In fact, as of the time of this writing, what we provide for our students would cost them over $10,000, and we're doing it for less than $3,500. Our Mission, as you'll learn, is to help our Associates complete transactions and to empower them to live the life of their dreams. We operate that way in every area of our business.

You'll need training. Our YouTube channel has free videos you can access right now. They won't make you an expert but will give you an idea of how things work. We release several videos per week on the channel for you, so subscribe now.

- Mondays: Motivational Mondays

- Thursdays: Q&A Thursdays

- Sundays: Deal Structure Sundays

---

We also have a podcast with several hundred episodes and growing. Please subscribe at **smartrealestatecoach-podcast.com**. After you listen, we'd love your rating and a review. After you rate and review, take a picture and email that to **podcast@smartrealestatecoach.com**, and you'll be entered into our weekly drawing for a free surprise gift.

Our website, **smartrealestatecoach.com**, has more start-up resources and a free webinar. Our *Quantum Leap Systems* home-study video course offers an insane amount of material for you, and it's not a one-time thing. This is a living, breathing course that we continuously update for changing times, evolving strategies, and changing laws, and a vital lifeline for anyone wishing to have success in the terms business. If you want to learn more, jump over to **getqls.com/now**.

The course comes with email support and a strategy call. It doesn't come with us actually working hand in hand with you, calling your buyers and sellers with you, and more one-on-one work that we provide in our higher-end Associate Programs, but you'll be equipped to go out and be the foremost expert in your area.

---

**"Yeah, but,"** you say, "I've seen other websites with other expert coaches offering different approaches, and I don't know whom to believe."

I can only teach what we as a company are doing. Find a mentor who is not just teaching but also doing deals—*currently*, because things change rapidly in the real estate market. Do some soul searching about exactly what you'd like to accomplish, then find someone who's done it. Also, some personalities obviously would fit you better than others. You will know that after watching two or three hours of their videos, and you can make an intelligent, informed decision.

If you've seen any of my videos, you've probably figured out there's no hype, and I'm pretty blunt and to the point (one of our core values as a company). If that's not your style, then I'm not the best mentor for you. You be the judge, because you can tell if you have a personality conflict with someone. I'm not so naive as to think I'm the only one teaching these techniques, but I know we produce deals at Prefontaine Properties—that's my goal, and that should be yours.

*I'm not so naive as to think I'm the only one teaching these techniques, but I know we produce deals at Prefontaine Properties— that's my goal, and that should be yours.*

Training should provide you a game plan of daily activities needed to support your goal. In our case, we know what our numbers are—the specific number of leads per week needed to produce our bottom line of deals per month. We have a team now, including **virtual assistants** who locate the phone numbers and dial FSBOs, Expired Listings, or FRBOs (pronounced "firbo") on a weekly basis, as do all our Associates.

We know how we got to this level, starting in 2013, part time, collecting our first check in September 2013, and two months later, with a little profit, getting our first virtual assistant. In January 2014, Nick started

### VIRTUAL ASSISTANT:

An outside contractor—either an individual or a company— that works off-site. Assistants work a set number of hours per week, using their own equipment for telephone and electronic communications, and are paid a flat fee with no worries about payroll and associated taxes and fees.

helping with marketing, and buyers started calling and emailing frequently enough that we hired a virtual assistant to call and screen the inquiries so I would have to talk to only those who were really serious. By December 2014, Nick became a full-time buyer specialist. A month later, I hired my first part-time in-house assistant to handle paperwork, and then Nick became our full-time buyer specialist. In 2016, my daughter, Kayla, and son-in-law, Zach, joined the team full time—Kayla as general manager and Zach as an acquisitionist. Kayla has since had two amazing, wonderful, outstanding, smart kids (I'm not a biased grandfather) and has limited involvement now and is greatly missed. My bookkeeper preceded all this and had been with me about nine years before we had to up-level that position and hire another full-time bookkeeper—as of now, an additional part-timer. Keep in mind, we run several companies, so that is not something you have to worry about right now. In fact, my CPA runs a done-for-you service to handle your taxes and your bookkeeping, knows the business integrally, and can be a huge asset for you. You can email **support@smartrealestatecoach.com** for his info or check our website under Resources.

Sometime in 2017, my son, Nick, and my son-in-law, Zach, pretty much took over all our buying and selling, and since that time they have outsourced and duplicated themselves with virtual assistants and apprentices.

The reason I shared this detailed timeline is twofold. First, we learned through experience how to scale up the staff and outsource only when we can clearly predict that the extra help is going to add to monthly profits by five to ten times what it costs. This is what we teach our Associates. Second, I want you to know that you can certainly be a solopreneur, but you can also grow a business and create a lifestyle that does not rely solely on you like so many other niches.

We can tell you exactly when you'll need to add which staff members and what to expect. Success does leave clues, and there's no reason for you to have to reinvent the wheel. You've got to remember to reinvest in yourself once you start doing deals, and you *will* start doing deals.

**"Yeah, but,"** you say, "real estate is volatile, and I'm afraid to be in a field where income might be very unpredictable."

Income is actually extremely predictable. If you come to me and say, for example, that you want to earn $100,000, I can tell you how many deals per year you are likely to need in order to accomplish that. We've determined how many leads are needed to produce a deal and what the average payout is. Eventually you will have your own numbers, but until then we have a good average based on our own business and our Associates all around North America. The average person can produce 5 to 10 leads a week as a beginner. If we know you'll need 150 leads to produce the $100,000 income you want and divide that by a conservative estimate of 5 per week, it's going to take you thirty weeks. So we can predict what kind of income might come from working two, three, or five days a week. We provide this to our students via a three-year, $1 million–dollar game plan worksheet. To get a copy of that for yourself, go to **smartrealestatecoach.com/3yearplan**.

**"Yeah, but,"** you say, "what if a recession hits again?"

Not sure what you mean by "what if." Of course it may hit again … and again. I'm not an economist, and I don't have a crystal ball, and I cannot predict economic cycles. If I could, I wouldn't be writing books and doing real estate deals. I'd have my feet up on a chair on the beach in the Cayman Islands. However, in my opinion, there's no better niche to be in regardless of how the economy is doing. When the market is flat, we're buying and selling. When the market is screaming hot, we're buying and selling. When the market is sliding backward, we're buying and selling. In 2013, when I started buying, everyone was doubting me and saying I was crazy. We amassed and maintain fifty to sixty properties at any one time now as they sell off and more come into our inventory. We can show you how to build your recession-proof muscles. This book doesn't have the space to do that, but as an example, if you have a ten-year term on a home, and your monthly payment is covered by your tenant-buyer in the home, and that payment is going 100 percent to principal over ten years, do you really care what the market does? All right, that was just to get you thinking, but we'll explore that together someday, and you can explore it yourself right now on our YouTube channel—don't forget to subscribe so you don't miss our newest and greatest recession-proof thoughts via video.

**"Yeah, but,"** you say, "I need even more income."

We have people come to us who are making good money—as a chiropractor, engineer, or police officer, for example—and can only get into this business if they can make upward of $300,000. We use the same formula so they walk out with a Business Game Plan that tells them how many leads they'll need per week and how to get there. For example, we know the average cash up front on these transactions is around $28,000, so six deals would provide $168,000, *not* including the other two Paydays. And our experience shows that everyone in our program should be able to do six deals in the first twelve months, and often more, by generating 180 leads total. That's not going to take long: less than five months, because even starting part time, as little as five or ten hours a week, our new investors are doing 10 leads per week. With the monthly cash flow producing an average of over $2,400 per month in income from six deals to support automation and outsourcing, we've seen plenty of people make the transition to doing terms deals full time in their first year. Please understand, we don't know you, your work habits, your history, or anything about you, so I'm using general timelines. If you want to manage your expectations properly, don't listen to the late-night infomercials, and do plan on six or even twelve months before your first deal. Then, I can tell you from watching all our Associates, the floodgates open, and your deal flow becomes quite automated, and your confidence skyrockets. And that can create a complete transformation for you—if you take the time and manage those expectations.

**"Yeah, but,"** you say, "my area might not have the same kind of seller or buyer prospects."

Your local market may be different—for example, if homes there are selling great in the conventional way. That doesn't mean you're out of business with doing deals the way we do. It means you're probably going to have to produce more leads than the average of thirty-five that we used earlier. A slow market may provide more expired listings for you to contact. And in any market, there are going to be people who experience life events—like a divorce, a death, job relocation, or retirement—that make them prospective sellers. There are also people who just refuse to pay a commission to a real estate agent. Residential buildings with two units tend to work great for our deals, because families are consolidating these days. Our techniques work on larger multifamily housing, too, and our QLS program includes a spreadsheet set up to do the math on whether such a deal will work. If multifamily housing is abundant where you live, you may want to expand what you consider your local market to capture more single-family homes to make your business more well rounded.

We live in a seasonal tourist area of Rhode Island with a permanent population in our hometown of only twenty-five thousand. The three-town island, called Aquidneck Island, is not going to produce enough business for us to do four to six deals a month. We expanded into Massachusetts, and when the market there started getting hotter, improving the ability for sellers to sell on their own, we expanded to Connecticut, which was still in a bit of a slump. You just have to look around you for the trends you can take advantage of or capture. There are plenty of towns or communities going through their own economic cycles. On the buyer side, because banks tend to be more and more difficult to deal with as far as qualifying for a loan, when you're selling on terms (rent-to-own or owner financing), you have an enormous pool of buyers. Regardless of your market or general market conditions, people will continue to get married and buy homes, downsize, upsize, and have life events. It makes single-family homes quite attractive for the investor.

**"Yeah, but,"** you say, "how can I possibly get all the necessary work done?" We teach about delegating, outsourcing, and scheduling in all that we do. We help you work on the high-payoff activities only. Thankfully, we're in an age when work can be outsourced to part-time contractors who can work on their own computers and other equipment from their own location. You read above about how we scaled up our staff gradually when it was clear the additional workers would generate more than enough profits. So much of this does not have to be hands-on once it's set up properly.

**"Yeah, but,"** you say, "I don't want to be a landlord."

Some people don't mind being a landlord and take on deals where they will have to run a multifamily building for some time before they can cash out. I will tell you that we work directly with buyers needing time to qualify, in single- and two-unit buildings typically. As buyers, they're responsible for all maintenance, repairs, and improvements. They treat the property and pay for the property as if they owned it. Dealing with these buyers rather than tenants in our properties alleviates the landlord responsibilities. We avoid three-unit buildings. And when it's four families and up, we use a management company to keep the units rented and deal with the tenants. In that case, our goal over time is to improve the net operating income numbers and sell it conventionally at a profit. What makes that possible is the way we buy the building without risking our own money or credit—on OUR TERMS.

In one case, we put down the equivalent of only one month's payment of $1,023. Another time, we were paid at the closing table to take over the property. You can do this by carefully timing your closing date to immediately after the tenant rents are due for the month. For example, we closed that property on June 2. Rents were due June 1, so the seller had to come to the closing table with all the June rents except the prorated amount for June 1—the only day he owned the building that month. Yet our payment to him (seller financing) was not due until July 15, after another cycle of rents had been collected. A limited liability company (LLC) owned by my individual retirement account (IRA) made the purchase and netted tens of thousands of dollars tax-free due to the timing. See appendix for a copy of the HUD Settlement Statement.

**"Yeah, but,"** you say, "I can't believe someone would give me a home or a building with no money down."

Our virtual assistant was calling around, talking to FSBOs. He found a retiring college professor who had a nice four-unit building with no mortgage. Running the building was a headache, and the owner needed money to pay for kids going to college. He was asking $259,900. I offered him the full price if he would take payments over forty-eight months before he would get a balloon payment of the remainder. We agreed on a monthly payment of $1,023. With 0 percent interest, the $259,900 principal was going down every single month for four years—for a total reduction of $49,104. So at the end of forty-eight months, I owed only $210,796. Our net cash flow every month was $735, what we cleared after paying the $1,023 and all the management fees, maintenance, heating, and other expenses. If you add the cash coming in every month, a little over $35,000 in four years, to the **principal paydown**, the profit from the transaction was over $100,000 (actually, this building has closed already at just over $116,000 net a few months short of the forty-eight months), a modest appreciation and profit in under forty-eight months. We may extend that term and gain more appreciation. We sold just prior to balloon-date time, but we could have even refinanced and kept the property if we wanted to—multiple options. The seller wanted his hands off the building immediately. Winter was coming. It's a very interesting time to make deals around our market—when the seasons are changing. Seeing a clear path to paying for his kids' education four years out was preferable to waiting for a conventional sale in which he might have taken a hit on his price.

**PRINCIPAL PAYDOWN:**

Paying in installments the outstanding balance of a mortgage that doesn't include interest or any other charges.

As another example, the office building that we occupy now was purchased owner financing—no banks, no signing personally on loans.

**"Yeah, but,"** you say, "what if the sellers change their minds before closing on a lease-purchase (sandwich lease)?"

We record what's called a notice of option or memorandum on the seller's title at the registry of deeds. This notice of option clouds the title, meaning they can't close on a sale without having a fee to us show up on their closing statement and having us literally sign off on it in order to convey with clear title. At the end of a term with your rent-to-own buyer whereby you've been collecting their monthly payment and paying the seller or their underlying mortgage, the buyer will close on the home, with their own new financing, directly with your seller. The bank's attorney or the seller's attorney will call you for the release, and you will stipulate your payment for that release (Payday #3). We've yet to have a seller "change their mind" at the end when either their loan was going to be paid off or they were getting a nice equity payment from it—why would they?

**"Yeah, but,"** you say, "the real estate market has ups and downs, and I'm not convinced it is a stable field to go into."

When buying on terms, like we do, you are in the driver's seat if the market changes. First, in all the examples I've given, there's drastic principal paydown every single month. In all the deals we do, there is no **personal guarantee of debt.** Your risk is the $10 or $100 you put up. In all the deals we do, it's possible to pick up the phone at the end of a term when the seller is due to be cashed out, and say, "The market has taken a drastic turn. I'd like to get an extension of twelve months, twenty-four months, or thirty-six months with the seller and the buyer," or "Let's adjust the price to reflect the market." Or you can assign the deal back to your seller. It's important that the paperwork on

**PERSONAL GUARANTEE OF DEBT:**

When you sign for a home mortgage, the bank requires you to pledge your personal assets to guarantee against default. A complete NO-NO when buying on your terms.

all the different types of deals, which we'll describe later in the book, and which we have in our QLS program, is designed around what I have just described. We've spent tens of thousands of dollars with our attorneys, and you can have access to all that.

• • •

We've covered a lot of the doubts that can become self-imposed road-blocks for those afraid to begin investing in real estate on their own terms. I was in a panic after I bought my first house this way, asking my mentor, "Now what do I do?" He assured me, "You will never be short of buyers." Sure enough, that first deal went through in eleven days. Imagine how it would be for you to know you can possibly have a check five to twenty days after securing a property.

Ever since we started, there might be two or three per year that don't get sold. Our contracts, "contingent upon us finding a buyer," provide for us to just say to the seller, "We weren't able to do it." There are no hard feelings. It's built into the contract. But it's very rare lately to not sell one of the homes, because enough people are having trouble getting a loan and/or saving for a down payment large enough to satisfy the banks. We've also renegotiated the numbers with sellers in order to make it more attractive to get sold or even lowered their back-end equity in order to start the payments without our buyer. There are all kinds of ways to adjust or change direction in these deals (we call that "pivoting").

We've lived through all the "Yeah, buts" and created checklists, forms, proper disclosures, and systems to handle them. We have videos on YouTube to help you get a feel for the deal structuring, the commonly asked questions, and a lot more. We like to show you how to deal with the good, the bad, and the ugly. The next chapter outlines the business process and how you become a transaction engineer.

# chapter 4

# NINE STEPS TO BECOMING A MASTER TRANSACTION ENGINEER

"You may not remember me," said the caller. I did remember him, but more importantly, he remembered liking what he had heard during a meeting my son and I had with him and his brothers seven months earlier. They had been liquidating an estate after their father's death and had a house to sell, which they ended up doing by using a real estate agent. A conventional home sale happens often in probate, because at least one of the heirs inevitably is eager to get cash right away.

The caller said he and his wife owned "another home here we'd like you to buy with owner financing like you suggested, and we've got to leave to go to South Carolina in four days, so we'd like to do this right away." Needless to say, Nick and I visited right away. The single-family home in Massachusetts had been listed with a real estate agent at around $200,000, but I estimated the value at $220,000. We ended up negotiating a purchase price of $183,900 with zero down. I will explain owner-financing deals in more detail in chapter 5, but basically the seller was going to play the role of the bank and take monthly principal payments of only $923 per month for forty-eight months, after which we would owe the remaining balance—but with no interest payments on the $183,900.

**EXIT:**

In our transactions, exit refers to how we're going to sell a property we control.

Our **exit** strategy, as always, was to find a rent-to-own buyer, which we did. The buyer agreed to pay $239,000 but would start by giving us a $15,000 down payment and paying us $1,500 a month in a thirty-six-month lease, which provided a buffer on our forty-eight months to cash out with the seller. So again we were getting 3 Paydays: $15,000 down was Payday #1 (we never take that small an amount anymore and have over the years significantly improved each of our Paydays, but this was early on in our business).

The difference between our paying the seller $923 a month and collecting from the buyer at $1,500 is a spread of $577 a month (less homeowner's insurance), Payday #2. And since the $923 a month was all paying down principal, unlike a traditional mortgage in which only a tiny piece of the early payments would have gone to principal, the profit on this deal after four years is around $128,000, including Payday #3—the final difference between the selling price of $239,900 minus the down payment, and what we owe at the end of the deal.

The homeowners got about the same price they would have gotten after paying a real estate commission in a conventional sale. With winter coming and their wanting to retire to the Carolinas, they didn't care that they were getting their price over time in payments. They had done their homework on us seven months prior and felt they could trust us. And importantly, we were able to buy on five days' notice and pay the seller's closing costs—a couple of thousand dollars. In those five days, we protected ourselves by doing a **title search** on the property and having the attorney process paperwork that the seller would sign, including giving us the right to call off the purchase or renegotiate if the property had any liens or other unexpected problems.

This owner-financing deal may seem like a quick transaction, but it actually illustrates the methodical Nine Steps to Success we introduced in chapter 2.

**TITLE SEARCH:**

A public-records check to ensure that the seller is the legal owner of the property and that there are no liens or other claims outstanding.

Update on this deal in this newly revised edition:

In year three, right before Christmas, we offered them $6,200 principal paydown for a twelve-month extension. They loved it because it gave them extra cash during Christmastime. We loved it because we pulled the $6,200 from another deal's Payday #1 and now obtained another twelve months (at $923/month) additional principal paydown. We did the exact same thing in year four, so now a four-year deal became six years. The fifth year we emailed and said, "We can offer you the same thing, or we can start new this year with a fifteen-year term but add 4.5 percent interest into the payment." They loved it, and their accountant loved it. So an initial forty-eight-month deal just went to twenty-one years!

These newer advanced techniques and longer terms are things we're doing these days to recession-proof our business, and we're sharing those of course with our Wicked Smart Community and Associates.

All nine steps are critical to any business. In the real estate world, if you were to miss one step, you wouldn't have a deal, because each step builds upon the previous.

## NINE STEPS TO SUCCESS

1.  Locating seller prospects

2.  Prequalifying seller prospects

3.  Using follow-up properly and efficiently

4.  Placing the seller in the proper bucket

5.  Structuring and presenting offers

6.  Following up on offers

7.  Signing or closing

8.  Locating buyer prospects

9.  Getting the property sold

## 1. LOCATING SELLER PROSPECTS

Any business is dead without lead generation, which for us means finding **seller prospects**. In the highly profitable Massachusetts home purchase at the beginning of this chapter, we were using expired real estate listings to generate leads and had located the seller more than seven months earlier when the family was selling a different house. I can tell you that between us and our Associates, I've seen leads call back one, two, and even three years after our first contact. Follow-up and patience in this business pays off very well.

**SELLER PROSPECTS:**

People who are likely to sell their property and are actively looking for buyers.

But let's take a more general look at how a business generates leads, regardless of the specific type. It involves training yourself (and then others) to systematically and automatically generate leads from the right places, but also being prepared to handle any lead that comes your way. And that involves getting the right information.

To be a transaction engineer, you have to find homes for sale, and the FSBOs are our top lead source in a flat or downward-trending market. They become a bit tougher in an upward-trending market, when homes are selling easily. You can find them online, like everybody else can. And obviously you can find them by

> *To be a transaction engineer, you have to find homes for sale, and the FSBOs are our top lead source in a flat or downward-trending market.*

spotting For Sale by Owner yard signs. People say, "Well, if they have a sign, they must also have an ad," but that's not true. Many sellers stick a sign in the yard as their sole means of marketing, which makes it one of the highest-quality leads you can get. We have a system that teaches you how to develop field agents looking for those signs. You literally have people driving around your market area looking for FSBO signs, because they are valuable enough leads that you can compensate them well for the information. We have a detailed report in our QLS Home Study Program that outlines how to launch your own field-agent program. You or they can find signs by driving a different way to work or to appointments. It can also be done by letting yourself get lost in areas you wouldn't ordinarily drive through.

Real estate agents put the homes they are selling on a multiple listing service. Those that have not sold are referred to as expired listings. These homeowners can be strong seller prospects if they are frustrated by the failure of their real estate agent. Expired listings have also been one of our biggest sources of leads, and similar to the FSBO explanation above, this varies with market conditions. Even in a very hot market, there are expired listings. They just tend to be more prevalent in a slower market, when Realtors aren't selling as easily. Please note that when I say "market," I don't mean that globally or even in a particular state. Despite radio shows, podcasts (I hope by now you've gone to **smartrealestatecoachpodcast.com** and subscribed and given us some five-star ratings!), and so-called experts talking about "markets," there is no one single real estate market. Market conditions vary greatly in North America as well as even in different areas within one state. We have outsourced calling these listings to assistants, but Zach and other team members are handling a lot of the calls, and I don't mind getting on the phone myself with "expireds" to stay on the cusp of the market. In fact, Zach has some new automation that allows him to get approximately twenty-plus leads weekly just from expired listings. In addition to VAs calling for us, we now use interns and apprentices for free, as do our Associates.

In addition to the expireds and FSBOs, we call on **FRBOs.** These are the same as FSBOs, only they are for rent by owner.

### FRBOS:

These are the same as FSBOs, only they are for rent by owner.

Direct mail is another great lead source. We use the yellow letter, which is in a handwritten font on legal-looking paper delivered in a small envelope that looks like it could be a wedding or birthday party invitation. The goal is to get the homeowner to open the letter. We also use postcards. For our few commercial-property mailings, we use a standard letterhead and business envelope.

The resource section of our QLS Home Study Program has contact information for the various companies we use to generate these letters and postcards, and for the list brokers who provide us homeowner addresses and phone numbers. Companies that specialize in real estate data are quick and easy to work with and can send a properly formatted mailing list directly to the company that produces and sends the yellow letter. Many other list brokers can be found by searching the internet, but you need to decide the target of your mailing.

Because lists can be broken down by price range and factors such as number of bedrooms or whether the property has a garage, we can focus a mailing on what we determine is our sweet spot. This will vary by market. We tend to focus on the $190,000 to $590,000 price range. Higher-end properties bring nice paychecks, but those within a couple of hundred thousand dollars in either direction from the market median sell faster. We also tend to focus on homes with three or more bedrooms. Your mailing budget and goals determine how much you want to narrow the list by categories. When I mention three or more bedrooms, that doesn't preclude you from doing two bedrooms. To this day, I have a home that I secured by lease-purchase that is a two-bedroom. About two and a half years into that deal, I converted to a purchase via subject to the existing financing. I still own the home, and it has well over $100,000 equity and is worth about $245,000. That's approximately six and a half years starting with zero equity, putting down $10 as my deposit, and not being on the underlying loan (still in past seller's name).

We have also had success with lists of homes with no equity, where the owner owes about what it's worth or even more, and homes owned debt-free. Either way, we have deal structures that would work for those sellers. Generally, the debt-free homes have produced much larger Payday #3s, because 100 percent of the monthly payments to the seller go toward paying down the purchase price.

Lastly, I'll mention a list that a lot of investors target but that we stay clear of: homes in or nearing foreclosure. Often these homeowners will tell you they don't want to sell, because at that point, they are focused on not losing their home to the bank. This is a list that can be worked effectively, but it's not my preference. If you decide to do so, you should consult a local attorney about complying with consumer protection laws, which increasingly restrict making contact with those homeowners. Alternatively, let those sellers find *you* via your website or other marketing, and you can deal with them case by case. Targeting any of these lists with yellow letters or postcards is just like any other marketing: you have to test it and then test it again until you get one absolutely cranking. If a mailing to a particular zip code or niche fails to produce a deal or minimum response rate, drop it or adjust your messaging and try again. We help our Associates set that minimum based on our history. We know that a mailing of 1,800 to 3,000 pieces always results in our buying at least one home—not a bad investment for the cost of about $1.25 per letter, and cheaper for postcards. While we get most of our leads by calling prospects, direct mail fills in the lead flow during the holidays, when phone response slows, and in early spring, when many people in our New England territory are selling conventionally.

A smaller source of lead generation is print and online advertising. Look for free classified ad sites in your market where you can run "I Buy Houses" ads. There are plenty of sites besides the well-known Craigslist. Calls from these ads are always trickling in, one to three a month, and you never know when one is going to be a hot lead. We recently got steady leads from an ad saying, "Local company looking to lease 3–4 homes in your area." We no longer run print ads, but they might be effective in a small or rural community.

We've recently been doing searches through real estate multiple listing services for phrases like "rent-to-own," "lease-purchase," or "owner financing," and that is bringing in leads as well. (Of course, it entails calling real estate agents, though this is made easier by following a script.)

After years of working with outside vendors in an attempt to best establish ourselves on the web, we decided to focus our efforts on doing these tasks internally. We've built a rather intricate real estate website with resources in place to ensure that we show up prominently on major search engines (like Google), and we've made this website template available to the Associates in our Wicked Smart Community. I can't quantify the results, but I believe that once you have cash flowing, it's worthwhile to spend some money on **search engine optimization**.

**SEARCH-ENGINE OPTIMIZATION:**

SEO is the process of editing your website or web pages in ways that help them rank high in the results of internet searches performed by people you are trying to reach, whether or not you are paying for ads to show up in search results.

We don't rely on one type of lead source, because having a variety of seller prospects is more likely to provide a constant flow of leads. Following the cliché advice of "don't put all your eggs in one basket," we constantly update our online resources with the most current lead sources.

## 2. PREQUALIFYING SELLER PROSPECTS

When we began discussing how to locate seller prospects, I mentioned that it involves getting the right information. Whether you or your team is calling prospects, or they call in response to a piece of mail, following a script is the best way to screen for those who are serious and motivated to sell— the **prequalified prospects**.

**PREQUALIFIED PROSPECTS:**

Motivated, prescreened individuals ready to do a deal on terms.

To this day, I remind even our most productive Associates that asking the right questions will help you determine a prospect's motivation and all the other information you need. This is a major teaching moment we take advantage of when we listen to and critique our Associates' live calls they send us.

> *To this day, I remind even our most productive Associates that asking the right questions will help you determine a prospect's motivation and all the other information you need.*

The critique of the live call shortens the learning curve dramatically. Our property-information sheets have our scripts built in, and our team uses and continuously tweaks them as necessary. We make those available in our QLS Home Study Program. (The cool thing about our course, unlike anything else out there in the real estate space, is that it constantly evolves. For example, when we update our scripts for our use, we update the course. When we update a form or agreement that we use, we update the course.) For example, depending on the situation, we might ask the following:

- "Is it by chance listed with a real estate agent right now?"

- "What is the asking price, and how did you arrive at it?"

- "Are there repairs and/or upgrades needed today that we should be aware of?"

- "If you were going to do any upgrades, what would you do?"

- "Why is it that you're selling?"

- "Is there a particular date you need to or want to be moved by?"

That second-to-last question comes nicely after the prospect tells you how great the home is. It's the most important question in revealing whether a prospect is saying "NO" or "no, not now" to a terms deal. Just listening and understanding why a prospect is selling is critical, because that will tell you if there's a huge motivation or if that person is just fishing around a bit. "When do you want to be moved, ideally?" is a question that goes with motivation and will tell you where you need to move ahead next in the conversation.

If it's an expired listing, a good question is, "Did you get any feedback as to why it didn't sell?" Again, let the prospect talk. He or she will talk. Whether that person blames something on the real estate agent, the market, or the buyers, he or she will explain to you what has happened so that you can then see how aggressive (or not) you can be about your price.

Of course, before we spend time asking most of the questions above, we make sure we are talking to serious sellers, not just any crazy callers. We direct calls generated by the yellow letters to a live virtual assistant for prescreening, since some people are just calling to say something like, "Why did you mail that letter to me? My house is not for sale," or "How did you know my house was for sale?" We've had some who suspected they were being scammed and called the police, who came to our office—and once to my home!—to investigate, and then had a good laugh and moved on. Don't let that alarm you—the main reason is because the letters work best if they contain no business card or formal letterhead; a few out of several thousand recipients are questioning.

Our virtual assistant will weed out the complainers, the curious, and the crazy and send us only the ones who seriously want to talk with us. That screening is done on a simple property-information sheet like all the other leads that our virtual assistant sends us. An initial call to those people usually takes just minutes. It takes about an hour to call and talk with, or leave messages for, the ten or twelve leads that a new investor typically gets in a week. Obviously there is then some follow-up needed from those calls and callbacks.

## 3. USING FOLLOW-UP PROPERLY AND EFFICIENTLY

Ideally the scripted questions on our property-information sheets—including "What do you owe? What are your monthly payments?"—lead to our asking prospective sellers directly if they will be open to having us buy on terms. If they say yes to terms, either lease-purchase or owner financing (or even subject to existing financing), then we have a formatted email that goes out with a full explanation of the terms, with the pros and cons of each option. If they say no to terms, we move on to another prospect but still have a system to follow up properly and efficiently. Each month, many sellers call back as a result of our automated follow-up, techniques we make available to members and partners.

Deciphering which leads to spend time on is very important. The information sheet may say that a seller said no to terms, but

*Deciphering which leads to spend time on is very important.*

what's more important are the answers that affect motivation: "Job relocating, six months; divorce, have to leave the state, two months; health reasons, have to leave the state, four months." Anything like that, we're going to very politely and professionally follow up and be there for them if they change their minds about selling on terms. Homeowners who put up a yard sign or place a FSBO ad online honestly think they can sell their home themselves, or they would not have tried. So you have to give them some time. Usually if you call them early in the process, it is going to take some follow-up. Just understand that, and don't be frustrated.

If we threw away all the prospects who said they were not selling or that they would not consider selling on terms, we would be throwing away hundreds of thousands of dollars. It's a truism in real estate that the money is in the follow-up. Life happens to people, and their circumstances change over time, which means their housing needs change. So we have scripts for follow-up calls to people who in an initial call rejected selling on terms. You can find these scripts and the email explanation of the terms in our online resources.

*It's a truism in real estate that the money is in the follow-up.*

As I was writing this book, I received a call from a homeowner I vaguely remembered. About a year earlier, he had been contacted as a result of an expired listing, but he said he was trying for sale by owner. He and I had three calls. He seemed like he was not a highly motivated seller but might be coming back to me in the future. So he went into the file system, which meant he'd get a routine form letter later, the last step before a file goes into the wastebasket. From that letter, he contacted us, I visited the home, and three days later we put it under contract.

These blasts from the past happen a few times each month, and when you consider the possible profit per deal discussed earlier, it's very expensive to throw them away.

In coaching new investors, we have found that they are pretty systematic about returning messages and calling back those who already have expressed some interest. The follow-up most often not done properly is with the prospects who say no. So we provide a system to make sure that follow-up happens automatically and no one falls through the cracks. The system is not high tech. You can create fancy spreadsheets and use elaborate computerization if you want, but in the past I simply put our prospects' property-information sheets into either a high-priority folder or a let-sit folder for follow-up and usually go through them weekly. Since then, my son, Nick, and my son-in-law, Zach, have automated a lot of what I had manually. I don't want to place links in here that will be outdated, but feel free to email **support@smartrealestatecoach.com** and ask them what our latest technology is and request related links.

If we can't convert a prospect to an appointment within three calls, we schedule that person to get a final letter, and then one callback three months later. We don't call again after that. We call the three attempts in three months our 3/3 System. If we have an email address, we use a database system to keep prospects on our email list until they opt out or reply that they've sold.

The goal isn't just to not waste a lead—but also to not waste time.

Even a new investor can accumulate at least ten leads per week, whether that be with your virtual assistant or on your own. So there are soon hundreds of leads. Throwing them into files the way I used to may seem archaic, but it worked for me. Our team and most of our Associates do use more automation these days, as I noted above. Speaking of automation, we even have automated dialers that leave a message with the push of a button and other systems that can leave hundreds of messages at a time, allowing us to only speak with sellers who are open to terms and want to speak with us.

By using our systems or similar, when you have motivated sellers, you will know when to call them—or you will get a callback based on one of your form letters.

## 4. PLACING THE SELLER IN THE PROPER BUCKET

During the previous steps, we have been asking homeowners about their willingness to sell on terms. We have in our scripts (you will read more on these in the next chapter) explanations of the different categories of deals, or buckets, as we call them. We can engineer different types of transactions depending on how much equity or debt the seller has and whether the seller wants to keep or relinquish the title to the property.

To place a seller in the proper bucket simply means figuring out the best way to structure a deal. All deals are different, obviously, but they fall into categories. We particularly like those in which we exit by finding a rent-to-own buyer. But we begin structuring our offer based on the outcome the seller wants. Each one of our buckets will produce a different result for the seller and for us. And this is by far the biggest learning curve for investors new to this niche. Eventually, you'll be a transaction engineer, of course, knowing how to navigate any deal. The beauty of being an Associate with us is we will be in the trenches with you actually doing these deals. There's no better way to learn how to navigate a deal and become a great transaction engineer than doing them with someone who has already done them!

## 5. STRUCTURING AND PRESENTING OFFERS

After determining what bucket you want to have the seller in, you must present an offer, attaching numbers to the structure of the deal. You can do that in person, on the phone, or by a combination of email and in-person or phone communications. We help our Associates lean on our National Community (**nationalpropertyteam.com**) in presenting the offer, so they have instant credibility.

We have found that some investors are wary of visiting the sellers' homes, but building rapport and credibility in person is important, especially in a difficult real estate market and economic climate. Sometimes all the conversations with the seller to that point have been handled on the phone, FaceTime, or Zoom, or by email. And even if both sides are comfortable, we send a team member to the home whenever possible. Of course, an in-person visit can get a little bit uncomfortable on occasion because you don't know what you are going to find.

We start by asking, "Is it okay if I take a look around?" And to keep it light, we say, "Do you have any animals, or do you have anyone that's not dressed?" Believe it or not, if we don't ask that question and sellers give us a go-ahead to walk through, we can run into surprises.

But going to the home has four advantages:

1.  We want to view it and not just rely on pictures online.

2.  The visit is an opportunity to go over all the questions and answers again, because there will be nuances where answering in person will build credibility. A key nuance involves being clear about exactly when payments are starting, which is often contingent upon us finding our tenant-buyer. Some other issues that may have to be settled are whether inspections are needed for lead, asbestos, or mold, and if so, who is responsible. These questions are part of structuring the offer because they affect the deal's bottom line.

3.  Sometimes the sellers may not disclose things properly or completely on the phone.

4.  We can have the seller sign the offer on the spot, although I will explain below why we don't always do that. We love using DocuSign or other electronic signature programs now.

Let's address working remotely, as that issue always comes up. You can work remotely and have a local person be your "boots on the ground." We've done that, as have our Associates. You may lose out on some deals where the seller needs (or thinks they need) to meet you in person.

## 6. FOLLOW-UP ON OFFERS

Follow-up on the offer is very simple after going through the previous steps. That means we gathered the right information, the prospect was prequalified, and we presented the offer without ambiguity, either by email, using electronic signature, or in person. The primary questions left to ask the seller are, "When are you planning on making this decision?" and/or "When is it best for me to follow up?" We don't want to be unsure of the seller's timetable or what is convenient for them, because then we can't follow up without risking bothering them. We'll get questions a lot about how and when to follow up. Just ask the seller!

Depending on the structure of the deal, we provide all the documents, forms, and agreements along with written and video explanations of how to utilize them in our QLS Home Study Program. In most cases, the forms and paperwork have been customized by our attorneys after hundreds of hours and tens of thousands of dollars invested by us.

## 7. SIGNING OR CLOSING

If we are taking control of a property by buying it subject to an existing mortgage or with owner financing, then we are headed to a closing similar to a conventional closing as far as title search, deal prep, and attorney involvement, as we're in primarily attorney-run deal states, and many of our Associates are in title-company-run deal states. If we are setting up a lease-purchase in which the seller is retaining the title, then it's not a formal closing, but we still must sign a contract and necessary supporting forms and disclosures with the seller.

Depending on state law, there may be no legal requirement to have an attorney at a closing or even a notary public at a lease-purchase signing. However, for liability reasons and to make sure all parties understand the process, we have a notary on our lease-purchase signings and an attorney for all closings, which also need a notary. To become a transaction engineer, you don't have to reinvent all the documents you and your attorneys need. You can download ours and adapt them to your specific state. One of the documents for the buyers to sign, if they do not get their own attorney, says they were offered the opportunity to have legal representation and that our attorney represents us.

Another reason we don't usually ask people to sign documents on the spot when we go to their homes is the ease and effectiveness of electronic signatures. We use an online provider, DocuSign, which requires each signer to go through each page and check off with initials that they read and understood it, which provides us extra liability protection, in our attorney's opinion. If someone is physically whipping through documents, they could claim later, "Well, I didn't read that," or "No one told me to read that," or "I didn't know what I was reading."

Note: If you live and operate in a state that typically has title companies doing closings, don't take that as your protection from a liability or lawsuit issue. You should always have an attorney on your site. I'm not an attorney, and this is not legal advice. It's simply how we operate, and it's my opinion.

## 8. LOCATING BUYER PROSPECTS

The easiest step by far, believe it or not, is finding a buyer for the property. Yet it's the step that haunts and scares new investors the most. They say, "Uh-oh, I tied up a property. Now what do I do? What if I don't get it sold? What if something goes wrong? What if I don't find that buyer?"

Chapter 7 of this book answers those questions, and we have a document called "The Buyer Process," which walks new transaction engineers through dealing with buyers—starting with their initial response to an ad and following through to the actual signing. Having successfully handled hundreds of buyers, my son, Nick, wrote this document to assist all our QLS students.

When I first started buying and selling property on terms, as soon as I located a prospective buyer, I had to stop all my other activities. It's an exciting time when you know you have a buyer with a check, but there's work to be done: the initial meeting, handling the forms with the attorney, and getting questions answered. Now we can continue generating leads while working with buyers. It's nice when you scale the business and it's running smoothly with or without you. Having gone through the entire process from solopreneur to a scalable team, I can tell you with precision how and when to do the same based on your goals and skill sets.

## 9. GETTING THE PROPERTY SOLD

The time frame for speaking with a seller, putting the home under agreement, and getting it sold can be as little as a week or—on rare occasions—as long as 120 days. It is usually less than 90 days, and that's very fast compared with conventional real estate sales. (No whining and complaining from real estate agents here, please! I know some of you can get it done quickly. I'm using averages.) If it goes past 60 days, we start looking at what the reason is. Usually it's the monthly payment. We can respond by lowering the rent-to-own price per month to the bare-bones monthly payment that we owe the seller. The idea is not to just break even but to bring in more buyer prospects.

As we meet with buyers, we help them work their monthly payment up if they don't have enough down payment, or we help them work the additional taxes due into the payment, preserving our Payday #2 cash flow. Ultimately, with the buyers getting in front of us and meeting in person, they are more comfortable working the deposit up with a plan—this is never something we try to push on the phone before meeting.

Another possibility is that we return to step 4 and restructure the deal. That change can happen at the request of either the buyer or the seller. Remember, everything is negotiable.

For example, we had a deal (the bucket we call Assign Out, covered in chapter 6) in which we signed a lease-purchase so we could find a buyer who we would then assign back to the seller to deal with directly. As time ticked away, the seller found a new home and wanted to move out prior to our finding a buyer, so the motivation had changed. The seller, worried about making mortgage payments on the home being vacated, called to ask about another option we had mentioned in an earlier meeting, which involved our guaranteeing the monthly payment as of a set date. We said, "Well, we can guarantee you a set date to take over your payments whether we have a buyer or not, if we restructure the terms to a different price." We cut in half the $32,000 back-end cash they were owed, adding $16,000 to our Payday #3. We did this because we were confident we would fill the home with our buyer prior to having to cover the seller's next mortgage payment or, worst case, prior to making more than one or two monthly mortgage payments of about $1,600 each. We did fill the property with a buyer prior to the first payment and collected over $40,000 in our Payday #1! So we profited from accommodating the seller's needs.

Here's what the seller had to say:

> *I was trying to sell my house on my own with no luck for two years. Chris Prefontaine met with me and explained my options on the house. Chris laid everything out on paper for me with no hidden fees or questions. After reviewing everything, I signed up, and in two months Chris had a contract with a lease-purchase ready for me to sign. Signed via email, and all is going smoothly. Very easy. Chris and his team did it all. Very happy; got what I wanted for the house.*

—Mike and Melanie S., Narragansett, Rhode Island
$395,000

The sale of the property completes our exit from the transaction, which we accomplish by systematically going through the Nine Steps to Success. The next chapter details what's involved in those first few steps.

## WHAT ABOUT COMMERCIAL REAL ESTATE?

The deals described in this book mostly involve residential purchases, but the business model works for commercial properties and multi-family as well.

While still in high school as a sophomore, my son, Nick, with money saved from washing cars in the neighborhood, invested with me in his first building—two commercial units that we rented out.

Then when the building emptied several years later we said, "Why not do exactly what we do on all our homes—which is sell it on OUR TERMS?" We did exactly that, to a window-supply company owner whose goal was to not use a bank. He has the master lease, runs the building, pays all the bills, and sends us a monthly check. He has a barbershop tenant in the other unit. We assigned our rights and associated lease for this barber over to our buyer, who put down $20,000 (and has continued to make annual $20,000 payments each July for seven or so years! Payday #1) nonrefundable, and whose monthly payment to us is $200 higher than our mortgage payments (Payday #2), while our mortgage principal is being paid down over $700 per month and climbing. Oh yeah, and our taxes are escrowed and included in our payment, but the new master lease tenant-buyer is responsible for all increases above a base outlined on day one.

We even had a property come to us once that had a commercial building *and* a home on it. The owners were elderly and didn't want to deal with it because the home was dilapidated. I said, "Well, I don't think it fits our business model, but what I will do is structure an option on your property for a price of $254,000. Then, as long as you're okay with it, I will bring it to market and see if I can get above that. I'll get the buyer, assign him or her back to you for an assignment/option-release fee, and we'll move on." (This was done using a simple-option agreement.) The deal didn't end up happening that way. But eventually, along came a couple, Chad and Lilly, who wanted to fix up and live in the back house and start a barbecue ribs business in the front. We structured a rent-to-own, just like we do on a single-family home.

We went back to the seller, who agreed to what turned out to be a very good deal for both of us. Unlike a conventional sale, it took a few years to get the cash-out, but he'd had no success with a conventional sale.

These nine steps can be mastered by anyone who commits to the path of learning. My son-in-law, Zach, had absolutely no experience and has become quite proficient. Enjoy his story and experience in the next chapter.

In chapter 5, I will share with you how simply solving challenges and providing solutions will create win-win-win relationships and 3 Paydays consistently.

*chapter 5*

# YOU CAN MAKE ALL
# THE DIFFERENCE

Working with the seller prospects you have located is really all about solving whatever challenges they are facing. These challenges are not always negative. We work with lots of sellers who are debt-free and looking for a better alternative. It is a totally different mindset from "selling" them on something. On the phone, your attitude and mindset is, *I'm here to fix their headache,* which could be debt relief, or changing the timing of the sales proceeds (on YOUR TERMS), or freeing them to move out of the area. But when a professional goes to help someone, as doctors, lawyers, and even lifeguards know, not everyone responds well. A master transaction engineer safeguards him- or herself against troublesome sellers by communicating properly and using proper legal agreements, or just by walking away.

I'm going to tell a couple of stories that may seem like bad scenarios, but they underscore the importance of never overpromising and being willing to walk away when you cannot structure a profitable deal that also solves the seller's challenges.

One story involves a completely rehabbed home in Shrewsbury, Massachusetts. The builder, who had fixed it up like new, welcomed a lease-purchase in which the buyer would have eighteen to twenty-four months to secure financing and, as such, would cash out the seller and us. We started sending buyers to look at the home right after signing our agreement, and the seller came back to us saying, "I really want six months." Well, that's not a realistic term for a lease-purchase, because rent-to-own buyers need time for credit enhancement.

We understood the builder's headache. He had invested heavily in the rehab. Winter was approaching, which in Massachusetts and many other markets is a time when people start to panic about getting a home sold. But we had explained the lease-purchase process, and the clear understanding was a term of eighteen to twenty-four months. So when he suddenly wanted to switch it to six months, I said, "You know what? This is not going to work. We're going to get our buyers angry. We're going to get you frustrated." So we walked away. We don't do as many AO (assign out) deals for this reason and because they only provide one Payday, but more on pros and cons later in the book.

The other story is all too common and involves homeowners who came to us because they were behind on their mortgage payments—in this case more than three years behind. Since the bank had not foreclosed yet, they were basically living in the house for free.

Based on what the house was worth and what they owed, they had no equity in the property, so it was not worth our taking it on.

Generally, we can't make a profitable terms deal with someone who is more than twelve months behind on mortgage payments—unless they have a lot of equity in the home that we can capture. New investors still establishing their cash flow should avoid these deals until they've built up enough scheduled Paydays #1, #2, and #3.

Will there be difficult sellers sometimes even after you've signed agreements? Sure. That's reality, as you'll learn more about in chapter 10. The legal agreements we provide our students, which we've spent tens of thousands of dollars developing over the years, protect us from deadbeats and litigiousness. But even with that protection, we don't really want to deal with someone who is going to be a headache.

There are so many leads in everyone's market that there is no need to deal with difficult people.

*There are so many leads in everyone's market that there is no need to deal with difficult people.*

## THE RIGHT SELLERS

Picture an old, historic tavern in a small city west of Boston that had been turned into a very large single-family home. It had been listed with real estate agents unsuccessfully at prices as high as $790,000 for over a year.

The most recent listing had expired and winter was coming, so the seller in Leominster, Massachusetts, was willing to sign a lease-purchase agreement depending upon what his price would be—have us find a buyer on OUR TERMS and stay in or assign that buyer back to him.

It took about four months, but we were able to find a buyer for $882,500 and get a $40,000 down payment, of which we retained $22,500. That was our only Payday because we had to assign the deal back to the seller, who began collecting $2,500 per month on the lease. Though we prefer deals with 3 Paydays, this was a great example of solving the challenge of a seller who owed nothing on the home and was able to wait for our lease-purchase to cash out within twenty-four months but just wanted to move out before the holidays, knowing the home was occupied through the winter. Someone else was paying about $1,500 monthly in taxes, utilities, and insurance, and making sure the pipes didn't freeze. We no longer do twenty-four-month terms on other deals—only AO. We also don't share that much deposit any longer with sellers. The typical percentage we share is 25 percent to 33 percent, depending upon the deal.

August through November is a very busy time for us to take properties under contract, because there is a perception among sellers that there are no buyers in wintertime. The market does slow down during the winter holidays, but there are always serious buyers out there for both conventional real estate sales and terms deals.

In our calls out to people with expired real estate listings, we got in touch with a couple in their late seventies. They were both real estate savvy and really understood the creativeness of terms buying. They had not only the property we called them about but also homes on the market in another state for about $475,000 and $675,000. Both homes were occupied by renters but had leases that were expiring.

With winter coming and the prospect of having to find new tenants, the couple was interested in what we could do. We were able to find a tenant-buyer for each home within about 120 days. Because the couple was real estate savvy, they chose to have us assign the buyers back to them. We collected up-front fees of $20,000 and $36,000.

They got the lease payments and were thrilled that both homes were then covering their expenses. Again, no Payday #2 and #3, but earning $56,000 from one expired listing call was not too shabby.

How important do you think it is to understand and master our scripts? Fifty-six thousand dollars important! Nowadays we do very, very few AO deals and focus more on owner financing (OF), sandwich leases (SW), and subject-to purchases (ST). We're also doing much longer terms. This helps build the recession-resistant muscles.

## WHEN FSBO FIZZLES

A lot of times when a real estate listing expires, the seller will *try* to take over handling the sale. I stress the word *try,* because 98 percent who try for sale by owner end up relisting with an agent or turning to someone like us to buy. Avoiding an agent fee sounds great in theory, and there are plenty of FSBO websites that encourage it. On the Zillow website, there's even a function that lets a seller set a Make Me Move® price. Some people get delusional and put a really crazy price in there, thinking it's just a number that they may or may not get. Potential buyers see the inflated price, see the house just sitting on the market for a while, and figure there must be a problem with it. The owners didn't know they were doing damage by throwing a high price out there, but the end result is an opportunity for a deal on YOUR TERMS.

Time is on our side in getting FSBO listings. Once the sellers have tried it for a while and gotten nowhere, they often respond to our follow-up messages. Remember from the earlier chapters: the money is in the follow-up with FSBOs.

## SINKING A BANK SHOT

Every week we run into homeowners who, sadly, have hit hard times—health problems, job loss, divorce, and so on. They try to talk with the bank and say, "We've run into trouble." All banks have what's called a loan-modification program, where they'll restructure the terms of the mortgage, sometimes lowering the interest, sometimes forgiving some principal while putting it on the back end of a loan, meaning when they eventually sell. They're all viable options, but too many times I'm running into sellers who had a true hardship and whose bank not only denied them a loan modification but dragged them out six, seven, eight, or nine months in the paperwork process just to say, "No, we cannot help you restructure this loan."

By that time, they may be even worse off, especially if they stopped making payments in anticipation of a loan modification.

That unmet need has created a huge pool of sellers we can offer solutions to. Banks also are forcing people out of their homes by doing this and then not foreclosing for many months, during which time the homes sit empty and in many cases fall into disrepair. That's another set of opportunities for you as the investor to buy a home on YOUR TERMS. This is one of a myriad of reasons why what we do is so super positive for all parties involved. We are creating generational changes.

Banks also have created two issues for buyers that have greatly contributed to our business success and the generational changes we're effecting with families around the United States. Since the 2008 debacle, banks have almost completely eliminated what they used to call stated-income loans, in which they wrote mortgages for people of means without the income verification of an IRS form W-2 or 1040 in the loan applicant's name. Self-employed people don't always report all, if any, of their income on the W-2 forms that employees receive each year from their companies. The buyers may have enough income, for example, but it's reported and taxed through one or more companies from which they draw cash that the bank won't recognize as documented income. Our rent-to-own programs give these buyers time to restructure how they report their income, which typically takes twenty-four months of "seasoning" before they can get a mortgage. A topic for another chapter and addressed in depth at our yearly events (**qlslive.com** and **bizscaling.com**) is the ability for you to sell your homes to buyers on owner financing, which completely eliminates the need for them to have a bank. This is a game changer and works well with our updated strategies, having to do with longer terms on owner-financing deals and more subject-to deals. This slight tweak to our model has dramatically increased the success of our recession-proof model and has helped even more buyers.

The second thing that has happened since 2008 (and continues to happen; this is a trending issue) is that banks have raised the bar on the down-payment percentage, credit scores, and other measures of creditworthiness, such as **down payment reserves.** These higher requirements have pushed a lot of buyers our way, because our program gives them time to repair their credit and save more.

## DOWN PAYMENT RESERVES:

How much money the buyer will have in reserve after making the down payment. A bank might require a mortgage applicant to have a reserve to cover six months of loan payments and insurance premiums. Generally, the money has to be accessible and not in a retirement account. Banks look at the money's "sourcing"—it can't just show up in someone's account as a loan from a relative—and its "seasoning," meaning how long it has been in the account.

## LIFE EVENTS, WITH OR WITHOUT STRESS

It should be clear from the stories in this chapter that some of our seller prospects had become financially overextended, but others were hardly stressed out, even though all were dealing with developments in their lives that necessitated selling property. The owners of the Leominster home and the older couple with rental properties were very well off financially and owed little to nothing on their homes. They just wanted to get a deal done and realize the best return financially. In this case, that was cash flow over time and best price—two outcomes not likely on the conventional market with a real estate agent or sale by owner.

Another example involves a building in my hometown that housed a tanning salon. A father and son owned the property. We contacted them because we saw a FSBO sign go up, and we then found out it was because the son had died recently. The father owned the building free and clear and was under no financial stress. But for financial-planning and tax reasons, it made sense for him to sell on terms rather than get paid all at once by a cash buyer or someone who would get an immediate loan.

Death, divorce, job loss, relocation, and other life events often figure into our leads that come to fruition. So, obviously, when we see that kind of motivation written on the property-information sheet, there's more urgency for us to pursue the lead, as they are seeking a solution as soon as possible.

## COMMUNICATING WITH THE SELLER

No matter how perfect a match the prospect is to our way of doing business, neither you nor I will be able to consummate a deal if the seller doesn't understand the meaning and pros and cons of a terms deal.

In the last chapter, we discussed our systematic follow-up, which includes scripted calls and ready-to-go explanations that we email to seller prospects. Learning to handle the sellers' reservations or commonly asked questions can be a challenge until you know the scripts, and that requires practice. When we first speak with many seller prospects about terms, their knee-jerk reaction can be negative or at least "I don't want to lease my property." Or, in the case of owner financing, "I don't want to get involved in being their bank."

To that we usually say, "Well, could you tell me what part of that you have a challenge with, just in case there's a misunderstanding?"

Almost always, the reluctant prospect has simply misunderstood what it means to do a lease-purchase or do terms, or has attempted it on their own in the past and failed without all our time-tested strategies, techniques, and legal forms. Sellers may mistakenly think they are becoming landlords, so the early stages of the conversation are geared toward making the possibilities clear: "If you got your full asking price—which you probably won't get on the open market—or got even more money, would you be open to hearing how we can get you there?" We explain we have different options, and most of the time they agree to hear us out. That's why the proper script and effective communication in the initial call are so important.

When we coach investors or take on Associates who are new at this, we emphasize the importance of studying and practicing the scripts almost like a daily workout. They also can listen in on our live calls to hear how the scripts play out with an actual seller, or they can listen to a recording later. And to take it to the next level, the Associates will have me or someone on our team or a certified coach on the phone with them and their sellers at the outset, so we are truly working the deal together. How many more deals do you think we could get working together than you could on your own, if I or someone on my team is calling your sellers for you and with you? We have our entire team (family) to help you, along with a growing team of amazing certified coaches. We also are 24-7 together on a private Slack channel with all Associates. The

> *When we coach investors or take on Associates who are new at this, we emphasize the importance of studying and practicing the scripts almost like a daily workout.*

learning and conversations that go on in there are worth ten times what any of our programs cost—simply invaluable.

For example, our Associate in Pennsylvania had a terms deal that had been agreed to in concept, but the seller had lots of questions that he was not prepared to answer. So he simply said he would call back with his senior Associate on the phone, and together we made a call that resulted in structuring a deal on a beautiful ten-acre, debt-free property worth over $400,000. Once again, the seller was under no financial stress but just wanted to move on to his next property and make sure this one got handled properly. That phone call led to a six-figure, 3-Payday deal.

## STICKING TO THE SCRIPT

We know our sellers and buyers have ten to fifteen questions they commonly ask. So we have scripted answers that our students can practice, master, and handle professionally. I can't think of any business that does not require (and benefit from) scripts for its customer communications. When you get a call from any telemarketer or visit a bank or store, they're scripted, whether you pick up on it or not.

When you sign on with us for the QLS Homes Study Program or as an Associate, the next step after you rehearse with the scripts is a training formula we call ACAA, which stands for the following:

> **Action:** *After you rehearse with the scripts, we want you to get on the phone and make your first three calls, which should be recorded.*

> **Critique:** *Let's critique the recordings. Did you say the wrong thing? Did you have no energy on the call? Were you totally off script? Based on that critique, let's make some adjustments.*

**Adjust:** *Next time, why not stick to using our information sheet and prepared answers for those commonly asked questions? Let's fine-tune how you handle your next set of calls, which brings us back to …*

**Action:** *Get right back into it and make some more calls, which we can also critique and adjust.*

I used this process in real estate long before I got into making terms deals. People who do this continuously become more efficient and effective. This goes for absolutely any task or skill set you're working on in business or personal affairs. A good example is my son-in-law, Zach, because he had no real estate background when he started with us, just a year ago at the time of this writing. The first two months of calls, he was stumbling through, just like new investors I coach often do.

Maybe the sellers didn't know, but I knew while listening for my critiques when Zach or our new investors were looking at their notes or fumbling for scripts. When I heard their first calls, I would cringe.

Five or so calls later, each one was like a new person on the phone as far as being scripted and superconfident. This is just one of the many benefits our Associates get.

After the calls became part of Zach's daily morning routine, he would send over recordings that could have been me or one of our experienced Associates talking. The practice showed up, and there was more of a natural flow to the conversations. My son, Nick, also started by practicing every single morning. He would literally chant the scripts. Once you've done it enough times, repeating the same thing over and over again, you will get better and be very well scripted. To this day, Nick follows a scripted format as our buyers specialist to make sure we are operating at the highest level. Luckily for every one of you out there in the amazing real estate business, we have a Live Buyers' Calls Program as well as a Live Sellers' Calls Program that you can purchase and immerse yourself in so that you are the superconfident investor speaking with them next.

A good way to practice is by reading the scripts as fast as you can over and over again, not worrying about intonation but just making the words become ingrained. By practicing answers to all the commonly asked questions, you are ready for one when you get it.

Some sellers ask only one or two questions, so it can take a while to get experience answering all the questions you need to be ready for. If you can role-play with someone on a regular basis, that's even more effective than chanting and practicing on your own.

If you don't have a mentor, or someone like us, to critique your recordings, you still should tape the calls and at least play them for yourself to critique. If you are thinking, *Man, I don't have any energy, I don't sound like I know what I'm doing,* then you know what you've got to do. You've got to go back and practice. It's an eye-opener— or, rather, an ear-opener—to hear yourself. And then (this is not an easy exercise), go ahead and play the recordings for someone who supports your goals and wants to see you succeed.

## THE POWER OF ONE DAILY DISCIPLINE CHART

For many years, I have used this Power of One self-accountability technique to get done what I know I want to accomplish for the year. If I need to master scripts, for example, I break down the goal into monthly, weekly, and then daily chunks. The Power of One is to put one daily discipline on a chart—"Practice scripts fifteen minutes"— and make myself check it off the chart each day for the week or month it takes. The inspiration came from a mastermind group way back in 1996. A participant named Mike said, "You know, achieving our yearly goals is really quite easy if we simply break the goal down to a daily goal and then do what's necessary daily. This will allow us to win each day, and by winning each day, we win the year."

## GIVING SUCCESS AN ASSIST

No matter how extremely well scripted you are, the person at the other end of the phone may have zero desire to listen to terms or no motivation to enter our kind of deal. If you don't recognize this, you're wasting your time, and you're going to be frustrated thinking you did something wrong. That's why we use the property-information sheets to assess who has the motivation to talk to us. We hit our targets by being systematic, not by changing the script each time a call goes nowhere.

As noted earlier, once we had the cash flow to pay for it, we began using virtual assistants to generate leads, so we would be talking to real prospects and have some advance knowledge of their properties and motivation. The assistants can be working from anywhere in the world but must be fluent in English and any other language widely used in your area. I have coached clients who said they had no success with virtual assistants, and we found the reasons were the language-barrier and time-zone differences that occurred because their assistants were in the Philippines, for example. Assistants should be calling sellers during the hours you specify, when you believe they will find the maximum number of people at home. We have been sharing our trained personal assistants with our Associates for a cost that we calculate should produce a minimum of one deal a month for a small weekly fee. We have since built that to a team of virtual assistants to allow them to not have onboarding fees or onboarding wait time with outsourced virtual assistants. Having them in-house now has shortened what we call TTFD (time to first deal). Shortening TTFD puts more dollars in your pocket more quickly.

I struggled with three virtual assistants before finding one I now have been using for more than three years. So I can help with advice on how to find and deal with these remote workers to make them most efficient. In addition to that, my son-in-law, Zach, is the one who has built an entire team of them. If you're not an Associate, you can hire the same people we used initially or find your own, and with the proper training, they will become an integral part of your team. If you decide to come on board as an Associate, you'll have the luxury and benefit of using our team.

## WHAT A GOOD LEAD LOOKS LIKE

A lead recently came in to our website for a property in Connecticut.

It was a referral from someone else we helped in that state. I called the homeowner, who said, "It's been on the market with an agent, Chris. It's about to expire. I've been paying my mortgage. I love my home, but I have to leave for a job in Syracuse, New York. So I can tell you, Chris, that I cannot make another payment." She said she had no equity in the home but was not going to walk away from it, because she wanted to protect her credit.

So I had a motivated seller who had debt and no equity in the home, which ruled out owner financing but meant I could set up a lease-purchase and fill the home with a tenant-buyer immediately.

Even if her real estate agent suddenly came up with a buyer on the open market, she would have to pay the commission and closing costs out of pocket. I could solve her challenge by providing a solution with immediate mortgage relief and no out-of-pocket cash. This deal was done without us ever meeting in person and with a quick visit to the home by one of our team members. We put it under agreement with a buyer from our list that very same weekend—with $26,000 down (Payday #1) over time, $410 monthly spread (Payday #2), and a back end (Payday #3) of over $41,000. One referral, one call, one nice property. A deal checklist in our online membership area includes reminders to get testimonials and referrals, the importance of which cannot be overstated.

• • •

To the right seller, I can make all the difference, and so can you. The next chapter goes into detail about the six buckets a seller might fall into, and when each makes sense.

# chapter 6

# THE PATH TO PROFITS: KNOWING WHAT DEAL TYPE TO USE

One of our Associates in Pennsylvania put a beautiful property under contract with the intention of buying with **owner financing**. That is one of the six buckets that we put sellers into, and as I mentioned in chapter 5, it basically means the seller plays the role of the bank. But there's a catch in Pennsylvania for our getting involved in that type of deal, because for us as buyers to purchase the property, we pay a 1 percent transfer tax, and we get taxed by the state again with a 1 percent tax when we sell. But we could get the same result for the seller by using a different bucket that we call the **sandwich lease**, and there would be no transfer tax up front, because when we start the process, it's a lease, not a sale, and the deed does not transfer. We moved the seller from one bucket to another. The seller didn't mind, and it saved us more than $4,000 in transfer taxes. There's another way to structure that, and that would be a contract for deed or install-

**OWNER FINANCING:**

When a property buyer finances a purchase directly through the person selling it.

**SANDWICH LEASE:**

A lease in which someone rents property from the owner and then leases it out to another tenant.

ment sale. But that's a bit more sophisticated and for another time. You may find some of those more detailed structured deals on our YouTube channel.

You've already read a bit about a few of the buckets, but I'm going to define each one and explain the pros and cons for the seller, the buyer, and the transaction engineer. In each category, we have spent thousands of dollars and hundreds of hours creating paperwork with the necessary protections for the investor. The forms are available in our QLS Home Study Program on Smart Real Estate Coach Academy.

## ASSIGN OUT (AO)

Assign Out means that as investors, we're going to contract with the sellers to control their property through a lease-purchase agreement, and then, once we procure the buyer with our right to do so, we're going to assign that entire package back to the seller to deal directly with our buyer. We then collect an assignment fee, or Payday #1, at the signing table with the attorney and buyer.

The sellers in this bucket retain ownership of their property because they're only doing a lease-purchase with us. So until the buyer cashes them out eventually, the sellers may see benefits in accounting for depreciation and getting tax deductions for interest, property taxes, and more. The sellers also keep any spread between what they pay out in a mortgage and what we were able to obtain from the buyer in monthly rent-to-own payments—so they get that Payday #2, not us. For example, if the seller's mortgage payment was $1,500 and we got a lease-purchaser at $1,600, the sellers would keep that extra spread of $100 a month. The sellers get most of the upside in this type of deal because we're stepping aside, not staying in the middle and collecting any of the profits. They also capture all their own principal paydown for their underlying loan if there is one. You'll see later that we capture all that principal paydown when doing a sandwich lease (SW). So the AO deal is not our favorite strategy. Why take only Payday #1 when you can have 3 Paydays?

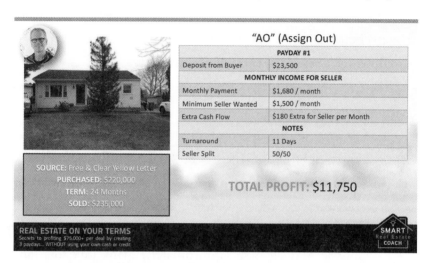

| "AO" (Assign Out) | |
| --- | --- |
| **PAYDAY #1** | |
| Deposit from Buyer | $23,500 |
| **MONTHLY INCOME FOR SELLER** | |
| Monthly Payment | $1,680 / month |
| Minimum Seller Wanted | $1,500 / month |
| Extra Cash Flow | $180 Extra for Seller per Month |
| **NOTES** | |
| Turnaround | 11 Days |
| Seller Split | 50/50 |

SOURCE: Free & Clear Yellow Letter
PURCHASED: $220,000
TERM: 24 Months
SOLD: $235,000

TOTAL PROFIT: $11,750

REAL ESTATE ON YOUR TERMS
Secrets to profiting $75,000+ per deal by creating
3 paydays... WITHOUT using your own cash or credit

SMART
Real Estate
COACH

Sellers with a mortgage can protect their credit by being assured that their payments are covered every month by the incoming lease payments. Some homes are overleveraged, or worth less than what's owed to the bank. That situation threatens a homeowner's credit if they need to sell. A sale for less money than is owed to the bank is called a short sale and creates a credit ding. This AO deal allows time for the homeowner to pay down principal on the mortgage each month, using money from the tenant-buyer's monthly lease payment.

Sellers who are not in that bind also benefit from an AO because they get an income stream with no real net cost. As in the deal in the last chapter involving a historic tavern, they just have to wait for a cash-out rather than get it all at once as they would in a conventional home sale.

If something goes wrong during the process—for example, a divorce or job loss on the buyer side—the sellers are now dealing with that directly. They can call back the transaction engineer to fill the home again, but in the meantime they might be making a payment or two, so that's the big potential downside for the seller in an AO. Or they can revert to selling the home conventionally. They may choose to do that if the market has increased since they started, which could lead to a good outcome.

There are four advantages for a rent-to-own buyer in this *or any of our buckets*:

1. A very quick approval process, as in twenty-four to forty-eight hours. There is no bank or loan committee to satisfy—just us, the investor who approves the deal. We use a service, which we recommend to our Associates, for prescreening buyers who need credit repair, as explained in the next chapter. Unfortunately, many investors (and educators) don't do this, and it may seem legal to them, but I don't think it's ethical or moral if not setting up the buyer to win. We won't accept a buyer if they don't pass all the tests or cannot afford the home in any way. Our model focuses on buyers cashing out.

2. Immediate occupancy if the property is empty. And even if it's not empty, occupancy usually comes within thirty days, unlike a buyer going to purchase a home and waiting forty-five to sixty days, or sometimes longer. We've installed buyers into homes in as few as three days—a day for a buyer's meeting and a day or two to arrange and complete the signing with the attorney.

3. No real obligation to buy the property. The tenant-buyer has set out to buy the home and has put up a nonrefundable down payment but technically has only an option to buy the property at some point within the term. Buyers who get a job relocation, win the lottery, or have some other big change that prevents them from going ahead can walk away and not be sued. They would, of course, lose any down payment that they had paid up to that date of default.

4. A big advantage is locking in the home price. Renters trying to save money and fix their credit can get priced out of an upward-trending market. In other words, home prices could rise faster than they could possibly save. In a rent-to-own, once buyers sign the deal, the price is locked, and just like a homeowner, they capture all the upside appreciation of a rising market.

For the investor just starting out, an AO deal is a good way to generate cash flow quickly, with little risk, in a simple transaction.

We gave an example earlier in the book of the very first deal we ever did—that took eleven days and had a nice profit of over $11,000.

The transaction engineer puts up no money and faces no credit risk.

The deal is easy to explain to a seller; as our students can learn in the scripts, it is just saying, "Let me take your home to my market and my buyers list and see what I can do." The transaction engineer is not signing on to make home repairs or mortgage payments but simply to find a rent-to-own buyer and assign back. There are no closing costs, although we always do spend a little money doing a title search to make sure there are no liens on the property that we're not aware of (that the seller may have forgotten to tell us about) or anything else that could deter a buyer from going forward.

Morally and ethically, even though it is the seller's responsibility once we assign the buyer, we don't want to place a buyer in the home if there are liens on the property not disclosed by the seller that could cause a problem later. In only one of our hundreds of deals, there was an old lien the seller had forgotten about, and he paid it off when it showed up in our title search. He thanked us, because the lien was accumulating interest as long as it went unpaid. It happened to be an old landscaper lien that he really did forget about, as he was traveling a lot for his work.

Several types of homes might be a good fit for the AO bucket:

- a home free and clear of any debt where the sellers don't mind getting paid monthly for a while but are just not willing to give up any spread or any back end

- a home where the mortgage payments are current but the sellers, again, are unwilling to share the sale profit with a transaction engineer

- a home with no equity, so there's no inherent reason for the transaction engineer to stay in the deal, but the buyer is willing to pay a sufficient premium to cover an assignment fee—as part of the price

- a higher-end home where the seller wants top price, and the transaction engineer is not comfortable taking on a high mortgage payment (or payment to the seller if no mortgage) and collecting from a buyer at that price level … if anything ever happened to the buyer, and the transaction engineer had to cover a payment or two—ouch!

- a home whose seller wants the shortest possible term

You'll see that in the other buckets, when we guarantee a cash-out period, we build in a buffer of time in case something goes wrong. If we have contracted with our seller to have a cash-out in thirty-six months, for example, we may be comfortable accepting a buyer with a projected twenty-four-month cash-out. With the AO, we're finding a buyer and assigning it back to the seller right away and retaining only an assignment fee.

### SANDWICH LEASE (SW)

In a sandwich lease, we're taking control of a property with a lease-purchase arrangement that gives us the right to sell the property, and we prefer to do so with our buyer in a rent-to-own. But instead of assigning the buyer back to the seller, we're staying in the middle of the deal. That's why we call it a sandwich. We're going to collect from the buyer and then turn around and pay the seller or, almost always, pay the seller's mortgage directly to the bank. The lease agreement sets a definitive date by which we guarantee our buyer is cashing out that property.

As of the time of this writing, Texas is the only state I'm aware of that does not allow a sandwich lease. There are other ways to operate in Texas, which we will discuss shortly. In fact, as of this writing we have several Associates in Texas.

A sandwich lease offers an investor the possibility of 3 Paydays. But if you are getting involved in such a deal, we advise you to have a protection in your lease agreement that allows you to decide when you start making payments to the seller or the seller's mortgage. We start ours thirty days after occupancy minimally, which guarantees us that we get to retain first months' payment from our buyer, adding to our Payday #1.

If it is a large payment that would keep you up at night, you should start contingent on finding your buyer first. If it is small enough, or you've done several deals in the market and you know you can sell the home quickly, or you already have a buyer who wants it, you could just specify a start date. Many of our properties are sold within a week or less because we have a waiting list of buyers.

---

## PURCHASE TYPE:
### SANDWICH LEASE

**TERM: 36 MONTHS**

**PURCHASE PRICE:** $324,500 MORTGAGES PLUS
$44,000 CASH AT CLOSING

**MONTHLY MORTGAGES:** $1765.55

**SOLD:** $434,900 AND $2,100 FOR 36 MONTHS

**PAYDAY #1:** $35,000

**PAYDAY #2:** $334.45 × 36 = $12,040.20

**PAYDAY #3:** $434,900 LESS $44,000 OWED TO SELLER
LESS MORTGAGE BALANCE AFTER PRINCIPAL
PAYDOWN OF $296,500 = $94,400

### TOTAL PAYDAYS: $141,440

---

## THE PATH TO PROFITS: KNOWING
## WHAT DEAL TYPE TO USE

Some properties that typically fit the SW bucket:

- homes that have no mortgage and a seller who is open to giving the transaction engineer good terms but doesn't want to relinquish the deed yet and doesn't need the cash right away

- homes where the seller is up to a few months behind on mortgage payments and has little equity. (It may be worth breaking the rule about you bringing no money to the table if catching up the mortgage arrears for the seller leads to enough cash out at the end in Payday #3. Catching up arrears is better done using the buyer's down payment.) As a general rule of thumb, we want at least two times the amount we put down as an adjustment to any equity that the seller may be getting at the end. We sometimes capture as much as five times. As an example, one of our Associates in Arizona had a woman leaving the state and asked us for $3,000 down for moving money. We settled on $1,800, but she was going to originally get roughly $20,000 at cash-out time. Instead we said we could give her $1,800, but we'd need $9,000 off the back end. So we invested $1,800 and knocked down the amount we owed at cash-out to $11,000.

- homes where the seller has no equity but the mortgage payment is so low that the buyer's monthly payment provides a spread of several hundred dollars for you to pocket monthly. (These add up. As of this writing, our monthly total spread—all our Payday #s—is over $28,000.)

- homes where the seller is current on the mortgage but doesn't want the responsibility anymore, and the home is move-in ready and has a nice low payment

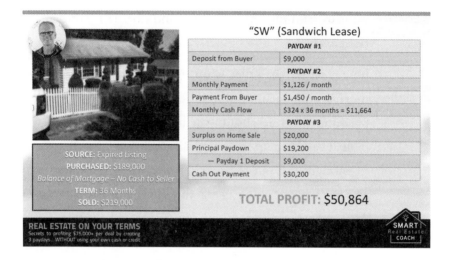

"SW" (Sandwich Lease)

| | PAYDAY #1 |
|---|---|
| Deposit from Buyer | $9,000 |
| | PAYDAY #2 |
| Monthly Payment | $1,126 / month |
| Payment From Buyer | $1,450 / month |
| Monthly Cash Flow | $324 x 36 months = $11,664 |
| | PAYDAY #3 |
| Surplus on Home Sale | $20,000 |
| Principal Paydown | $19,200 |
| — Payday 1 Deposit | $9,000 |
| Cash Out Payment | $30,200 |

SOURCE: Expired Listing
PURCHASED: $189,000
Balance of Mortgage – No Cash to Seller
TERM: 36 Months
SOLD: $219,000

TOTAL PROFIT: $50,864

REAL ESTATE ON YOUR TERMS
Secrets to profiting $75,000+ per deal by creating
3 paydays... WITHOUT using your own cash or credit

SMART
Real Estate
COACH

We had a deal involving a family with a home sitting empty in Rhode Island, as they had moved to Massachusetts and had lost their renter. Winter was coming, and several months had passed in which a real estate agent had failed to sell the home. The agent felt bad because the husband was in Baghdad, Iraq, serving his country as a civilian contractor, and the agent thoughtfully called us to see if we could help. The husband reviewed alternatives we presented and went with us, lease-purchasing the home, procuring a buyer, and assigning that buyer back to the couple to deal with. But I had some concerns about how that AO deal was going to work while the husband's job was keeping him in Baghdad most of the year. The wife, living on her own, would have to deal with any problem that arose with the home.

I explained that the sandwich lease would mean 3 Paydays for us and a little less money for them, but they would be 100 percent hands-off the lease-purchase and related buyer cash-out concerns.

They agreed to be moved to the SW bucket so they wouldn't have to worry mentally or financially about the lease-purchase, which we guarantee.

Another example that shows the possible advantages of the SW bucket to the seller involves an elderly gentleman. I made an offer to him to sell us his home on owner financing, which we're going to talk about next. He said, "I really love what you guys are doing. I studied up on you guys. I researched you online. I used to be in finance in the car business, so I get what you're doing. I want to do this, but I've got to run it by my attorney." His attorney talked with us and advised him that it was much safer if he lease-optioned us the property for the same price, with the same monthly payments— but retained the deed. So we structured a sandwich lease and placed a buyer in the home. We agreed to pay him $1,200 a month that would go 100 percent toward principal, meaning it was reducing our cash-out and maximizing our Payday #3.

In Texas, if you take control of a property by lease-purchase and find a buyer, you can assign it back to the seller. Or you can control the property via a "subject-to" purchase and then lease it to the rent-to-own buyer. In that case, you actually purchase the property, **subject to** the existing mortgage, and then sell it to your

**SUBJECT TO:**

A seller transfers the deed to the property subject to the existing debt staying in place and remaining in the seller's name.

buyer on owner financing or just rent-to-own. You just can't stay in the middle of a sandwich-lease purchase under Texas law. You can also buy with owner financing and then sell rent-to-own. You just cannot do a lease on each side of the deal. Please note that we are not attorneys, and laws can change without our knowing, so you'll want to consult with your attorney, especially if you are not in our Wicked Smart Associate Community.

Sellers may gain several benefits from a sandwich lease. If they are trying to qualify for another mortgage for a purchase elsewhere, having a lease-purchase, not a rental or an empty home, helps maintain their credit. A sandwich lease avoids the **due-on-sale clause** contained in all mortgages, so the sellers still have a mortgage sitting on their credit. Whether a bank will qualify them for another purchase obviously would be determined by their credit history, income, and other personal information as well as the bank's policies—but at least they have an agreement with a definite cash-out on their current mortgage along with monthly payments being covered.

**DUE-ON-SALE CLAUSE:**

The terms of the mortgage forbid transfer of the property without fully paying off the mortgage.

Sellers in a sandwich lease retain the tax advantages of home ownership until cashed out. This means they will depreciate their property while still on the deed.

From an accounting standpoint, you are simply recording lease income in and lease payment out as an expense (whether it's a mortgage or a direct payment to the seller). The seller with a mortgage gets debt relief with a lease-purchaser taking over paying the mortgage. And depending on the structure of the deal, the investor may pay closing costs that a seller normally incurs in a conventional sale.

The sandwich-lease bucket generally provides investors the 3 Paydays—cash from the down payment, monthly cash flow, and the profit at the end. We like this bucket for most of our deals. When it's time for a formal closing, your buyer would be closing directly with your seller, and your company or land trust would be listed on the closing statement as an option-release fee or whatever the underwriter (lender) decides to list it as. This is because you would have recorded a notice of option or memorandum of real estate (you basically are clouding the title, ensuring that the property cannot be sold without your sign-off), so you are protected. One of the reasons this is so important is that the seller will now see how much you're making and could possibly get a bit greedy (or what we refer to as a seller getting amnesia) and want some of that—especially if your deal was originally that they get nothing or little out of the deal. The other issue with a sandwich-lease closing at the end is that you will have to track down the sellers and have them sign the deed to get this closing done.

## OWNER FINANCING (OF)

For you as an investor, owner financing means you buy the property and the seller plays the role of the bank, carrying back a mortgage on any balance due. This arrangement works well for free-and-clear properties in which the seller doesn't want to get paid all at once. The big difference between sandwich lease and owner financing is that this deal involves the transfer of the deed from seller to investor at closing.

All of the owner financing we've done has been structured with **principal-only** monthly payments. As the months tick away, our exposure lessens, so even in a market downturn, these deals are phenomenal. We can fill the home with a rent-to-own buyer, but because we own the home, we

### PRINCIPAL-ONLY:

Principal is the amount borrowed in a loan. Banks structure home mortgages so that most of the monthly payments in the early years cover interest charges, and the loan recipient only gradually begins paying off the principal. An owner financing deal can allow for all payments to be 100 percent principal.

also have the option of selling payments with owner financing to a buyer. We stick with rent-to-own because if they default, the result is an eviction. If buyers default after you sell them property with owner financing, you have to legally foreclose, which is much more expensive than an eviction in most states that I'm aware of.

Sellers typically get a premium price for owner financing while delaying or spreading out any capital gains. By taking principal-only payments, they don't have to report any interest income, which is taxable. Currently, as I write this book, interest rates are so low that interest doesn't make much difference in these deals. We also pay the typical closing costs associated with a seller because we're not offering down payments and we cannot expect them to pay out of pocket to sell us a home that is debt-free.

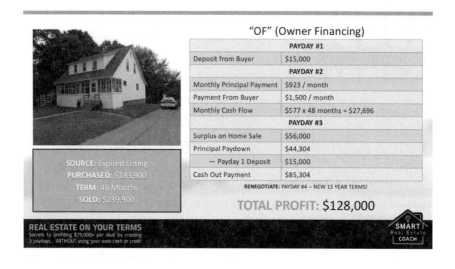

| "OF" (Owner Financing) | |
| --- | --- |
| **PAYDAY #1** | |
| Deposit from Buyer | $15,000 |
| **PAYDAY #2** | |
| Monthly Principal Payment | $923 / month |
| Payment From Buyer | $1,500 / month |
| Monthly Cash Flow | $577 x 48 months = $27,696 |
| **PAYDAY #3** | |
| Surplus on Home Sale | $56,000 |
| Principal Paydown | $44,304 |
| — Payday 1 Deposit | $15,000 |
| Cash Out Payment | $85,304 |
| RENEGOTIATE: PAYDAY #4 -- NEW 15 YEAR TERMS! | |
| TOTAL PROFIT: **$128,000** | |

SOURCE: Expired Listing
PURCHASED: $183,900
TERM: 48 Months
SOLD: $239,900

REAL ESTATE ON YOUR TERMS
Secrets to profiting $75,000+ per deal by creating
3 paydays... WITHOUT using your own cash or credit

SMART
Real Estate
COACH

Since you own the home as the investor in an OF deal, you pay for insurance on the house, unlike the AO or SW deals, where the seller has to maintain insurance. That sounds like a drawback, but it actually lowers costs in the deal. We share access with our Associates to an investor-friendly carrier that provides much better rates than an individual homeowner would pay to insure a non-owner-occupied house. In a lease-purchase, the seller switches from a homeowner's policy to a landlord policy and requires the tenant-buyer to maintain renter's insurance for belongings inside the home. If the investor controls the deed, he or she must maintain landlord insurance.

Typically, the OF deals have a balloon payment due to the seller at the end of a term—for us, often forty-eight months. The legal forms we use allow for that term to be renegotiated if necessary or desirable.

For example, if you have a rent-to-own buyer ready to cash out, you can offer to cash out the OF seller early in exchange for a discount.

A 10 or 15 percent discount makes for a very profitable deal for the investor and is fair for the sellers because they have the option to take it if they want the cash now rather than waiting another year.

You as an investor must be comfortable with any OF terms, because you are obligated to make payments on the home you bought or the seller can foreclose and take back the property. You've also got to be comfortable with how you prescreened your tenant-buyer in the home and make sure that buyer has enough down payment so they're not going to back out too easily. With all buyers, we evaluate their "skin in the game" by looking at the size and source of the down payment. For example, if the source was borrowed money, they could have less of a challenge walking away—defaulting on you—than if they used their own funds.

We had a deal (still have it) that started as an owner-financing forty-eight-month term. We knew the tenant-buyers were having trouble with financing and considering moving on or just renting. This forty-eight-month deal already carried a nice $120,000-plus profit all 3 Paydays. One December we offered all our owner-financing sellers a payment toward principal of $6,200 in order to extend our terms another twelve months. They gladly did it (who wouldn't want extra cash during the holidays?). The following December they actually asked if we were interested in doing it again. We did. This forty-eight-month deal now turned into a sixty-month deal, and we picked up another approximately $24,000 in principal, turning a roughly $120,000 profit into over $144,000 in profits.

It gets better.

We are now structuring longer terms in an effort to be more and more recession resistant. We took that same deal this past year and suggested to the sellers that they change the terms with us from principal only to interest of 4.5 percent and push the term out fifteen years. They came back and said their accountant loved it and asked for ten-year terms. We said it had to be fifteen, and they accepted. An original term of forty-eight months now was a twenty-one-year deal. We often combine strategies, so that gives you a taste for how lucrative they can be as well as how creative you can get.

We recently purchased our office building, moved our companies into it instead of renting, and inherited some great tenants. We did it with owner financing—twenty-year terms. That's for all of you out there thinking this can't be done in your area. We live on an island, and most would comment that owner-financing deals cannot be done there. They can be done everywhere.

## SUBJECT TO (ST)

In this bucket, a seller transfers the deed to the property to the investor subject to the existing debt staying in place. In other words, the seller's mortgage doesn't go away. It is not paid off or assumed by the investor. It remains in the seller's name. As an investor, you have agreed in writing to make payments on a home you now own to a loan that's still in the seller's name. As you can imagine, this bucket can sometimes be difficult for sellers to embrace if they don't know you. Yet we do several of these deals each year, and they've been done for many years around the country. Banks can't stop a transfer of a deed.

One potentially cumbersome aspect of the sandwich lease is that when the lease-purchase term ends, which could be as long as nine years later, the investor has to track down the seller to sign over the deed. A strategy we have used after having a sandwich lease in place for about a year or so, having built up trust and credibility in the relationship by making our regular payments, is that we ask the seller to transfer the deed, moving the deal into the ST bucket. Sellers may agree because of the trust factor or because they want closure.

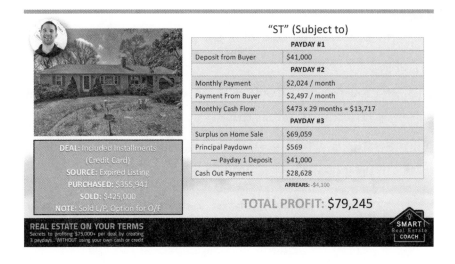

| "ST" (Subject to) | |
|---|---|
| **PAYDAY #1** | |
| Deposit from Buyer | $41,000 |
| **PAYDAY #2** | |
| Monthly Payment | $2,024 / month |
| Payment From Buyer | $2,497 / month |
| Monthly Cash Flow | $473 x 29 months = $13,717 |
| **PAYDAY #3** | |
| Surplus on Home Sale | $69,059 |
| Principal Paydown | $569 |
| — Payday 1 Deposit | $41,000 |
| Cash Out Payment | $28,628 |
| ARREARS: -$4,100 | |
| **TOTAL PROFIT: $79,245** | |

**DEAL:** Included Installments (Credit Card)
**SOURCE:** Expired Listing
**PURCHASED:** $355,941
**SOLD:** $425,000
**NOTE:** Sold L/P, Option for O/F

**REAL ESTATE ON YOUR TERMS**
Secrets to profiting $75,000+ per deal by creating 3 paydays... WITHOUT using your own cash or credit

SMART
Real Estate
COACH

We've done many where they are leaving the state and want to get the paperwork done first.

Earlier we discussed how every mortgage has a due-on-sale clause, in which the bank requires its loan be paid off before any transfer of the home occurs. But a federal law, the Garn–St. Germain Depository Institutions Act of 1982, says a property can transfer to a family member or trust for estate-planning reasons without triggering the due-on-sale clause, so those kinds of transfers are happening regularly. In our experience, as long as banks are getting their payments, they are happy to take the checks and are not calling back any of the hundreds of loans in the ST transactions done by us, our Associates, and the students we coach. The risk for the seller lies in the investor not making payments. We do, by the way, take title to these in a trust we create using the seller's last name and the street address, giving it the look and feel of family estate planning for the transfer.

The positives for you as an investor are the following:

- You have no deadline to exit the deal—no balloon payment due.

- You have full control of the property and can place your own insurance.

- You bought a home with no credit check, and the loan stayed in the seller's name.

- You don't have to chase the seller down years later to get a deed signed over.

- You write off taxes, interest, and depreciation as the owner of record.

## WHOLESALE

When you, as an investor, take control of a property by way of any of the deals described previously and then assign your contract to another investor, that's the wholesale bucket. The other investor must fulfill the contract, while you pick up an assignment fee. It might range from $5,000 to $20,000, although that high end on larger homes is not too common. Some investors make a business out of wholesaling. We don't, because we want ongoing cash flow, not small checks from one-Payday transactions that we'd have to do again and again.

Though we don't look for these deals, we had one recently where the seller insisted on a cash purchase despite our offering a higher price through a different bucket. We put the home under contract with the full understanding that we were going to find someone to step into our shoes. As far as the seller was concerned, she had a cash sale that would happen on or before a specified date. We found a rehabber who did exactly these types of deals. The rehabber took over, and we received a $10,000 wholesale-assignment fee. It's one of the buckets you can use to exit a deal you're not comfortable with. Having sold a hundred homes per year as a Realtor, I simply prefer NOT to have one-Payday deals and instead have 3 Paydays for every deal that simultaneously create wealth.

## OPTIONING

Placing an option on a property is a simple one-page agreement with a seller to buy it at a certain price. Let's say you're contracting to buy a home at $200,000. You agree with the seller to pay a $100 nonrefundable fee for the option to have a sixty-day or ninety-day window to find a buyer, just like wholesaling, to step into your shoes to then close the contract.

You, as an investor, can use an option for privacy if you close on the property and then sell it as a separate transaction, since the seller won't see the details of the profit you're making. You close with the buyer and simultaneously cash out the seller. An alternative that we prefer is to discuss openly with the seller how you are engineering the transaction and why you need a notice of option recorded to protect your interest. Then the person taking over the option can close directly with the seller, and you will be paid an option-release fee that's not a surprise to the seller.

*You, as an investor, can use an option for privacy if you close on the property and then sell it as a separate transaction, since the seller won't see the details of the profit you're making.*

We option a property about once a year. It happens when we are very unclear what price we can get for the property or how fast we can get it, or because it's exceptionally high end and we're just not sure how the market's going to react. We might put an option on it for thirty or sixty days and tell the seller we're going to take it to market and see what happens.

The wholesale and optioning buckets are very similar, and both are alternatives for sellers who want cash right away and won't agree to the longer terms of the other buckets. It is, however, a bit crowded in that niche (competitive) and not nearly as lucrative as our TERMS deals.

## MINIMIZING INVESTOR RISK

Our business started with almost all AO deals, and now we do almost all SW and OF transactions. The AO deals carried less risk of our making mistakes because the lease-purchaser became the seller's responsibility. Over time we realized that in the SW deals, we could put away the monthly spread, Payday #2, in our reserve account.

That covers us for the occasions when life happens to some tenants and collecting becomes a headache once or twice a year out of our fifty or so deals. The legal components of our SW agreements allow us at any point in the term of a contract to assign that contract back to the seller without his or her consent, so there's no huge risk unless you didn't listen to me and made a down payment in the deal.

On an owner-financing deal, you as the investor have two ways to avoid foreclosure if you are not taking in the money necessary to cover your payments. You can renegotiate amicably with the seller, just as you would do in asking a bank for a loan modification. Or if they won't negotiate, you could deed the property back to the seller.

We haven't had to deal with that type of situation, but we make a practice of being proactive whenever we anticipate any problems with buyers.

While the choice of buckets depends on the seller's circumstances, we have seen above that it also can benefit buyers, who are the subject of the next chapter. My son, Nick, has become quite the master of the entire buyer process and completes not only all our deals with our buyers but also hundreds of deals with our Associates. Imagine having him in your corner while you work on your deals. He literally "finds" extra dollars in every deal he digs into. I know you'll enjoy his chapter.

# chapter 7

# OKAY, I HAVE THESE PROPERTIES— NOW WHAT DO I DO?

*By Nick Prefontaine*

After all the hard work of FINALLY acquiring a property on your terms, reality starts to sink in. The thought starts bubbling up in a new investor's mind: "Oh, crap. What if it doesn't sell? What do I do? Where do I start? I don't know the first thing about marketing a property, never mind talking with buyers. What if I say the wrong thing, or what if, worse yet, no one even calls?" Rest assured, getting the phone to ring is the easy part. Once the market sees that you are offering a home "rent to own," the floodgates open. Just think of it—there's only 20 percent (roughly) of the market out there who can walk into a bank and get a loan today. The other 80 percent are sitting on the sidelines because they don't know there is a path to home ownership that you're able to provide.

Roger is one of our Associates in Atlanta, and I'm going to highlight him and one of his deals. The lead was an expired listing from Roger's virtual assistant. The sellers had pumped about $70,000 into the home with the hope of cash-flowing it with Airbnb. If they were to sell on the open market, they would lose at least half of that. That's where Roger came in and was able to offer them a solution. We were able to locate some great buyers that had family already in the area. Paydays were as follows:

- Payday #1: $32,852 ($30,000 down payment + first month's rent)

- Payday #2: $4,968 ($207 spread every month x 24 months)

- Payday #3: $17,013 (principal paydown + premium)

Total Paydays = $54,833

As I mentioned earlier, there's roughly 20 percent of the market who can walk into a bank and get a loan today. Now, that number might be higher, but the potential buyer will get killed with interest and points and other costs, because they represent a higher risk to the lender. For our purposes, let's go with 20 percent. That means there is another 80 percent of the market out there who is not able to get a loan. I'm not saying that they are all good; however, there is a portion of that 80 percent who have the money saved for the down payment and make great incomes. They are sitting on the sidelines while they save up the 20 percent for the down payment or until their credit scores increase. Those are only a few of the reasons. In addition to that, we see things such as divorce, death in the family, relocation to a new area, self-employment, or any combination of those, and that will hinder buyers from getting approved for a loan. Out of all those buyers, we are looking for deserving buyers with good down payments. That is a key stand-alone phrase that we use in all our ads. What does that mean? Exactly what our program is all about—a down payment of 3 percent to 10 percent, and we make sure that their household monthly income is at least three times the monthly price of the home. This way we attract buyers, not tenants.

I specialize in the three most important activities involved in our own deals and in working with Associates and their buyers to maximize their down payments. These are the following:

1. Calling and reviewing applications to schedule buyer meetings

2. Conducting buyer meetings

3. Coordinating the attorney signing. This third step is crucial because it is where we and our Associates get paid.

The Buyer Q&A videos educate the buyers, and we usually require them to have seen a video or two before we even get them in to see the property. Those videos say that we need a down payment of at least 3 percent to get in the door, but we try to get them into the range of 7 to 10 percent or more when we talk with them. If they can put 10 percent down, we know we have someone strong. We call this down payment the first of our 3 Paydays, but it can extend out over time if the investor is willing to take it in installments. Where does this extra money come from? Typically, on the call to review their applications, we find out that they have money coming for their tax refunds, bonuses, or 401(k) plans that they would like to commit toward their down payments. It's important that buyers name their own plan that they are comfortable with.

When a prospective buyer has sufficient funds for the down payment and a plan to get there, we'll meet with him or her. Once we get the buyer meeting set up, we'll get them over to our tenant screening. In addition to the regular tenant screening, we find out how long it will take them to become "mortgage ready." The vendor we use specializes in credit enhancement. He also used to be a mortgage broker, so he knows the underwriting rules and regulations, and he will talk with the buyer by phone, review credit history and personal situation, and tell us the pertinent information about when the buyer will be mortgage ready. We put all our tenant-buyers through this intensive but inexpensive screening—fifty dollars per person, which the tenant-buyer pays for. We require that for all our buyers. If the buyer balks at paying the fifty dollars per person for the screening with no guarantee that they'll get the house, that's probably not someone you want to work with. Then our agreements require them to participate in the credit-enhancement program.

We are almost always accepting or rejecting buyers purely on financial criteria, as a bank would. To a new investor, this is an important point, and you should familiarize yourself with antidis-crimination laws nationally and where you live. Our training videos explain what criteria we use and how we put that in writing for buyers we reject. We had to reject a buyer who recently had been in jail for a cocaine convic-tion; it showed on the criminal check, which is part of the screening.

> *We are almost always accepting or rejecting buyers purely on financial criteria, as a bank would.*

As a reminder, buyers are not always struggling with credit enhancement. Many buyers just need time for a myriad of reasons that we'll discuss—they have a down payment, and they have a good to great credit rating.

On the other hand, we accepted a buyer recently who had one little ding on her criminal history. We chatted with her and decided we were comfortable that she had just been in the wrong place at the wrong time as a young teenager.

Before we make the final decision to accept buyers, they meet with us. We live in Rhode Island, the smallest state in the country, and on an island within Rhode Island, so we have to do business in a broader area across New England. Some of our buyers are as much as a two-hour drive away from us. But we've never found buyers, if they are serious, having any problem driving that distance to meet us or come to our attorney's office, because they're so excited to have this program—and their meeting us is just as important as our needing or wanting to meet them.

At the meeting, we go over a "buyer letter of intent" that they sign. It signifies that they understand their down payment is not refundable once they're accepted, and they are taking the home as is and accepting all responsibility. The letter lets them choose whether they are performing inspections or waiving them. We always encourage buyers to give themselves that option for their protection.

Because they are signing a lease, not closing on a home purchase, attorneys are not required by law to be present. But for clarity, and for everyone's protection, we treat it like a closing. We have them sign all the documents in front of our attorney after we accept them.

They need to understand that concerning possible repairs, it's just like they bought the home. They can't call us about a clogged toilet or a leaky roof. An exception to their being just like a buyer is that they cannot buy a homeowner's insurance policy until the home is in their name, but they must buy renter's insurance, which is inexpensive. Whoever is on the deed pays for the homeowner's policy, so we cover it. However, the buyer legally must fulfill any requirements of that policy, such as having smoke alarms. We require all our tenant-buyers to supply proof of renter's insurance before they take occupancy of the property.

## TENANT-PROTECTION LAWS

(We are not attorneys and recommend that you seek out a local attorney. However, this is based on our experience.)

Whether a lease-purchase buyer can take advantage of state tenant-protection laws to override the purchase-option language in our contracts is a gray area. Almost every lawyer we have asked said courts probably would find that the lease-purchase agreement can't force rent-to-own buyers to waive rights that they would otherwise have as a tenant. Frankly, we don't want to become the test case, so we try to fix any situation that comes up rather than have a judge decide our buyer has become our tenant.

Case in point: We had a family with four children move into a home we had bought subject to (ST) the existing loan.

The seller disclosed no knowledge of lead paint, but the family did a home test, later confirmed, showing there was lead. Since the seller got out of the home under economic hardship, it fell to us to pay to mitigate the lead-paint hazard. That decision was right from a tenant-law standpoint. We could have dragged the family into court based on agreements our buyers sign that say they take the home as is and our honest disclosure that we had no knowledge of lead, but morally, ethically, and legally, we felt the right thing to do was to have the walls and woodwork stripped and repainted or covered over according to state lead standards. We later learned that the seller had been dishonest with us and the home was registered with the town as having lead paint. That case caused us to update our agreements, putting the responsibility for any lead mitigation, mold, or asbestos back on the seller. If the seller has no money, however, what do you do? Well, you can avoid all this by doing proper inspections up front on your end before deciding if you'd like to go forward. It costs a small sum of money to avoid having to pay a fortune down the road.

This is just one of hundreds of small adjustments we make to policy and agreements as a result of being in the field and actively doing deals. This benefits our students and our Associates immensely.

## WHEN LIFE HAPPENS

A buyer couple who were engaged when they signed the papers later told us they had broken up and could not afford the home without both their incomes. They said, "We're sorry. Here are the keys back. We can't fulfill our obligation." We ended the deal amicably and retained their down payment.

There are two sides to that coin. A couple who had a few kids together bought one of our rent-to-own homes a few years ago. Last year we received a call from one of the parties asking to be removed from the lease because they had broken up. Due to the fact that they both signed the lease, we have to keep both parties on it until the other party gets their own loan and cashes us out. Life doesn't stop because someone breaks up. We've been lucky, but if they decide to stop making payments, we could go after everyone on the lease. Once again, we do this for our protection.

Another buyer said, "My father-in-law had a second heart attack (way out of state in Chicago), and we're leaving, and here are the keys." Unfortunately, those life events come up once or twice a year to cut short multiyear deals. We refilled those homes with buyers who were stronger and had larger down payments. That can happen because our list of buyers grows over time as we market our homes, and sometimes we have multiple applicants for one home.

If a rent-to-own buyer is unable or unwilling to take out the mortgage to cash out a deal, he or she may ask to just stay as a tenant.

Typically we give a nice sixty- or ninety-day notice to vacate, and they can become someone else's tenant. For example, a couple who paid regularly asked to get out of a lease-purchase because they were expecting a child, unexpectedly. We said, "Just make sure you give us a sixty-day notice, and we can refill the home." They were thrilled because they thought we were going to hold them to the years they had left in their lease and to a potential purchase. We had enough time before our balloon payment to the seller was due to simply put the home back on the rent-to-own market. If the due date had been closer, we could have sold the home outright, still at a profit. But our analysis showed that our profit would be far better if we let the term continue, as it was a good deal with principal-only monthly payments.

## THE BUYER PROCESS IN DETAIL

When buyers inquire, whether by phone or email, I always direct them to call me to arrange a viewing. I never set up viewings over text or email. Once I get them on the phone, I tell them, "Our rent-to-own program isn't a good fit for everyone. First, to see if it's for you, see the *How Does Rent-to-Own Work* video on our website. If it is still a good fit, you can call me back to arrange a viewing." You'll find a lot of buyers prequalify themselves out once they learn that it does require a down payment, AND THAT'S A GOOD THING! We actually now have a completely automated system including texts, voice messages, and emails. This is all built out and is available to our Associates. Again, why reinvent the wheel?

We place a lockbox on vacant homes so we can give a buyer a code for access. I'm very clear with all buyers that they lock and secure the property after they see it. I tell them that we have police driving by the home, and I don't want to get a bunch of calls from them that the house and/or lockbox is wide open. When our sellers still occupy a home, they serve as our partner to walk the potential buyer through the home. I'm super clear with our partner (seller) that he is just there to walk the potential buyer through and point out property-specific things. Don't go over numbers or the program. That goes both ways, as I tell the buyer that the seller's sole function is to walk him through. He doesn't control the numbers. If the buyer has any questions on the numbers or the program, they can circle back to me. More importantly, if they are interested, they can fill out the Next Step forms and get them back to me.

Simultaneously, I email the potential buyers our Next Step forms. I say to them, "After you view the home, if you are interested in taking the next step on this property, please fill out the forms and get them back to us." These forms have been crafted and tweaked over the years so they ask the right questions and give us the important things we need to know. They are also crafted to get the highest possible down payment, which helps us but also puts buyers in a better position to get their financing at the end of the term. (Remember, we're setting people up to succeed.) After I get those forms back, I'll call the tenant-buyer to go over that information. I start off by asking them questions about their work and employment history. This also will warm them up to me and make the rest of the call easier. Typically we want to make sure that they make enough to support the home. For that we are looking to make sure their monthly household income exceeds three times the rent. If they don't make enough to support the home, there's no reason to go over their down payment.

However, as long as their household income exceeds three times the rent, I will move into the down payment section of the forms. I'll say, "Hypothetically (I can't convey tone here, but imagine the 'if you ever' kind of tone), if you were to buy a home, how much do you think you would have set aside for a down payment?" I promise you, 80 percent to 90 percent of the time, their answer will be HIGHER than what they wrote on the Next Step forms. My goal is clarity on where the payments are coming from. The forms we use list several sources—retirement accounts; tax refunds; and other assets, such as a car they might think about selling—to get the buyer thinking about where they could get money for a down payment.

Suppose it's going to take a buyer two years of credit enhancement to get to a point where they are able to get a mortgage, and they expect a $10,000 tax refund every year. We'll see if that buyer would be comfortable committing, for example, $7,000 of that refund for three consecutive years. It's important at this stage to make sure the buyer is telling you a number, so that if there's ever a challenge paying, it's not a number you came up with. So in this example, by calling and speaking with the buyer in more depth, we're able to get an extra $14,000 out of that conversation (Payday #1 in installments).

(Important point here: All of this, including scripts, calls with actual buyers, as well as actual Buyer's Meetings, are in module 6 of our QLS Course. Pick that up today to accelerate your growth.)

If we come to a point where we're comfortable with a buyer's income and down payment, we're going to go ahead and schedule a meeting. As soon as it is booked, we get them over to **screenthetenant.com** for their tenant screening. A typical conversation goes like this: "Now that we have our meeting set up, I'll give you the info for your tenant screening. Go to screenthetenant.com, and pay the fifty dollars per applicant for your screening. If you want to show us how serious you are about this home and this whole process, you can take care of this right away. That way, by the time we meet, we'll have your screening back, and we'll know how long we have to give you with the lease to become mortgage ready."

## TESTIMONIALS FROM BUYERS

*"We have been working with Pre Property Solutions for a year now out of Oxford, MA. My husband and I had been searching for a new home and were tired of renting but did not have the credit qualifications or confidence of knowledge to enter the home-buying process. Once we found Pre Property Solutions, our lives were greatly changed! After meeting with the team and getting into the home we loved in such a speedy yet thorough process, we were also surprised at the quickness of home repairs prior to us moving in, including a new kitchen counter and sink. Once we were approved, all efforts were made toward getting us in the house ASAP. It all sounded too good to be true from the get-go, but it was very true and very good! We signed up for the credit repair program, and our credit has improved immensely, as well as our knowledge on continuing to keep a respectable credit report. The PPS team is kind and genuine about providing an opportunity to those willing to work hard to their goals. We will be forever grateful for this experience and for the services Pre Property Solutions provides."*

—Amber and Tim

*"After a bad divorce and a foreclosure looming, I thought I would never be able to buy a home again. Pre Property Solutions made it possible, and now I am living in my dream home. Easy to work with. Communicated with me throughout the process."*

—Michele

*"Pre Property Solutions made our experience of getting into a home easy and hassle-free. They were there to answer any questions we may have had and made the experience very positive. We got into our home within a few weeks, and they went above and beyond—truly an amazing group of people. Thank you, Pre Property Solutions, for getting us into a lovely home!*

*"We had such a great experience with Pre Property Solutions! We found a home and were able to finish the process and get in the house in as little as three weeks! We are with our kids snuggled on the couch in our new living room, grateful for everything they've done to make having a home possible!"*

—Jason and Kristin

*"After a divorce and hitting roadblock after roadblock when trying to buy a new house, I was referred to Pre Property Solutions by my brother-in-law, who stated they were great to work with. I contacted Chris and began the process. Once I found a house, everything moved quickly and smoothly. Chris, Nick, and Susan not only answered all my questions but did so in a very timely manner. They made the process easy and stress-free. I think the biggest thing for me was that I was not made to feel guilty because of my credit status. Instead, I was assured that many people are in my position, and the thought of owning another home was not impossible but more probable and attainable. I would and will definitely recommend Pre Property Solutions to friends and family. It has always been my dream to buy a big, old Victorian home and restore her to her original beauty, and because of Pre Property Solutions, I am now living my dream."*

—Anonymous

*"My husband and I were stuck. We owned a property that we couldn't immediately get out of, for many reasons. This forced us not only to become landlords, as the town house no longer met our needs with one-year-old twins, but also to move twice in three short years. We wanted so much to settle into a community that our children would grow up in. We came across Pre Property Solutions when searching for yet another rental.*

*"We called and spoke with them, and I found myself excited and scared all at the same time! Could this be real? Very skeptical but curious, we pursued this home, and we are so happy we did! Chris and team made it happen for us! They held my hand through the entire process. They worked within our particular situation, and it happens fast! We will be moving into our beautiful new home, within a fabulous school district, next week! More than that, Chris bought our town house with their lease-to-own only weeks after we signed on our own property! He set it up so that the timing for purchase, on both ends, works perfectly for us. I'm guessing that, as you read this, you'll find yourself very skeptical, as we were. My only advice is to take the time to check it out and talk with Chris. You won't be disappointed!"*

—Anonymous

## MARKETING TECHNIQUES

We post our properties first and foremost on our website and then email them to our list of buyers before advertising anywhere else. Our homes often sell to buyers on our list before the public even knows about them. Then we post to online classified services, social media, and other real estate websites where buyers are looking.

I tell our new Associates, "It may sound trivial, but get associated with your chamber of commerce, and get associated with your

Better Business Bureau immediately, because people are checking that right away." We realized that our Associates in the US were having more of a challenge getting accredited by the Better Business Bureau if brand new to the real estate business. As a result, we now have a letter that goes out to them connecting them with National Property Team (**nationalpropertyteam.com**) and sometimes speeding up the process and acceptance.

> It may sound trivial, but get associated with your chamber of commerce, and get associated with your Better Business Bureau immediately, because people are checking that right away.

I joined both organizations (chamber and BBB) after an incident in 2013. One Saturday morning I sat in my office waiting for a buyer who was driving ninety minutes to see me and had even confirmed by phone that he was on the way. Eventually the buyer's uncle, an attorney, called, saying, "I checked online, and you're not even a member of the chamber of commerce or Better Business Bureau." He had told his nephew he suspected a scam and not to bring me a check. Thanks to that wacko call, we have been an A or A+ rating accredited member ever since. I want to thank those people who throw curveballs at us, because it sometimes helps us improve our business.

We have experimented in our marketing with different business models within the real estate field. For several years we bought properties near colleges, either conventionally or on terms, and rented them only to college students, whose parents cosigned. It was very profitable; the properties paid themselves down, allowing us to exit with a conventional sale over time.

We also recently released training information for our Associates on land-only deals using the same terms we use for homes. Some people want to build a home but don't know how to begin or can't get the conventional financing that requires 50 percent down on the land. We are partnering with builders to offer what becomes a finished product. That business model opens up a new buyer pool and profit center.

In some of our Associate relationships, we offer an exclusive territory, perhaps three or four counties, where nobody else from our team or other Associates will be competing. If someone else has been in the market teaching or practicing sales on terms, our attitude is that there's still plenty of business out there. Some of the strategies we use have been around long before we started, but we are constantly evolving the strategies and setting up the systems to support our business based on actually doing deals—not just teaching about them. We have seen an enormous challenge in the real estate education niche, and we call it "the gap." The gap is the time between when a student takes a course or attends an event and the time he or she actually gets a deal done and realizes profits. Part of our mission as a company is to help Associates do more deals while simultaneously decreasing the time to first deal (TTFD). For your sake and your family's sake, don't blindly follow someone teaching real estate but not doing deals or someone who did deals years ago and no longer does. That's a recipe for disaster, with the market forever changing and evolving.

In dealing with our buyers, we live and learn, just as we do with our sellers. So every time we have a challenge, we tweak the system to handle that, and our new investors have access to those improvements, which is invaluable. In the next chapter, we explain why we can say our systems are proven and predictable.

Here's another deal that one of our Associates did in North Carolina.

Should you take on a property that's been listed for THREE years?

This might sound like a death sentence to most Realtors. But not if you're an investor in the terms business!

What if you ran across a house that has been on the market for THREE years? Should you go in on it?

Most people would say no. But in the terms business, you're not catering to the same market as a Realtor. So in many cases, we're able to sell houses that otherwise wouldn't sell—and we can make a solid Payday when we do it.

In this case, one of our Associates did take on a house that had been on the market for three years. And guess what? He sold it in seventy days.

Let's take a look at what happened.

*From three years to seventy days.*

This particular home was owned by a military family who had been forced to relocate. They had gone through a lot of hassle and had plenty of headaches with this property, including two evictions with two different attorneys, maintenance issues, repairs, and renovations.

The house had been on the market for three years, and they were starting to wonder if it would ever sell.

This property was a FSBO (for sale by owner) that our Associate acquired through a postcard. Now, it's important to note that when we send out mailers, it's very different from what other real estate professionals do.

It's not uncommon for a wholesaler to spend thousands per month on mailers. I was just talking to someone who spends $5,000 per month for all his mailing—and that's even on the lower end.

We don't spend more than a few hundred dollars per month on mailers—if we even do them. In this case, our Associate spends around $150 per month on mailers, sending out about three hundred postcards in total—and this is his twelfth deal, so it's clearly working for him. Other Associates spend zero on mailings, as they get more than enough leads from the other sources we teach (primarily expireds, FSBO, and FRBO).

Getting back to the deal, it was set up as a sandwich lease with a thirty-six-month term. This is a fairly short term, but it can still provide a great 3 Paydays if you manage it correctly.

The owner of the property originally had it on the market for $340,000. But over the course of three years, they had brought it down to $285,000! Our Associate ended up purchasing it for $300,000.

Now, you're probably wondering why he purchased it for $15,000 more than their asking price. This is something we often do when sellers are hesitant about rent-to-own deals. It gives them a nice incentive and shows them that we are serious about these deals. And since we're getting so much of our profit from the principal paydown, it doesn't put a huge dent in the final Payday.

It's just one more reason why terms deals can be beneficial for the seller, the buyer, and the person structuring the deal.

The other part to remember is that the seller isn't exactly getting $300,000 in cash. When we structure these sandwich-lease deals, what we're really doing is promising to pay off their mortgage and pay them the difference. In this case, the seller had $248,000 in underlying debt on the house. So our guarantee was that we'd pay off that debt and give them $52,000 in cash.

One thing we also make clear from the beginning is that we're receiving the principal paydown when we're making payments on the house. This just makes logical sense. When the seller makes payments, they get the principal paydown. But when we make payments, we get the principal paydown. This also means that when we're paying off the mortgage in this deal, we're paying a lot less than $248,000— which is where much of the profit comes from.

Explaining these two concepts right from the get-go and making sure everyone is 100 percent clear is absolutely necessary for any terms deals. That way, you don't run into a roadblock or misunderstanding a month down the line.

And there is one final lesson with this deal. As mentioned above, the seller had many problems with tenants, evictions, and attorneys over the course of the three years it was on the market. When it came time for us to find a buyer, we were getting calls from the owner telling us to make sure we didn't rent it to this or that person because they'd had trouble with them in the past.

Here's what we told the seller: "We're not looking for renters! We're looking for buyers."

> *People run into problems with terms deals because they end up dealing with renters, not buyers.*

People run into problems with terms deals because they end up dealing with renters, not buyers. They don't put down payments in place, they don't screen their buyers, and they have no way of verifying that their tenant will actually be able to buy the home at the end of the term.

Our process takes care of all those problems by weeding out people who are just looking to rent and focusing on people who will be mortgage ready by the end of the term or sooner. That's why we're able to be so successful with these deals—because we know that the buyer is an actual buyer, not a renter.

## THE PAYDAYS

Let's take a look at the numbers on this property. We already mentioned that our Associate bought it for $300,000 with $248,000 in underlying debt. He was able to turn that around and sell it for $359,000 with a thirty-six-month term.

Payday #1 is the down payment, which ended up being around 10 percent, or $36,000 in total. Half of that ($18,000) was paid up front, and the rest was paid over the next four months.

Payday #2 is the monthly spread. Normally, that means the difference between what you're paying to the owner and what you're getting in rent from the tenant-buyer. In most cases, that's a few hundred dollars per month.

In this case, however, there was no monthly spread. The tenant-buyer was paying $2,000 per month, and all of that was going to paying off the mortgage and paying down the principal. To people who read our articles frequently and keep up with our deals, this might come as a surprise. Sometimes we have small monthly spreads, but rarely is there no monthly spread whatsoever.

But don't worry! We always tell our Associates and our audience that the real money comes from the principal paydown. The monthly spread is a great bonus, but it's not the end-all be-all—and this is a perfect example. The principal paydown shows up in Payday #3.

Payday #3 made up the bulk of this deal, coming in at right around $43,000 in total. And that number is calculated by taking the sale price of the house ($359,000) and subtracting the purchase price ($300,000) as well as the down payment ($36,000). That leaves you with $23,000 in profit from the sale.

But there's still the principal paydown! In this case, out of that $2,000 monthly rent, $555 was going to paying down the principal. As mentioned above, we get all that principal paydown—so when you multiply it over thirty-six months, that's another $20,000 in our Associate's pocket.

All in all, that's a total of $43,000 for Payday #3 and a total of $79,000 for the entire deal.

(If you're paying very close attention to the math, it's actually $19,980 for the principal paydown and $78,980 for the total—but we're not going to stress out over that $20.)

And there you have it: $79,000 on a house that had been on the market for three years, sold in seventy days.

Imagine if a wholesaler or rehabber tried to make this deal happen. They couldn't come close! They would have had to give such a low offer that it would have been an insult to the seller.

We were able to help this owner sell their home for more than what they were asking and get a family into the property that otherwise never would have been able to purchase it.

This type of stuff only happens in the terms business, and that is truly what makes it so special. Wholesalers and rehabbers = 1 Payday. TERMS = 3 Paydays!

Congratulations! You now have a solid foundation in buying and selling properties without using your own cash or credit. Now the fun begins, and we can start to talk about building and running a successful real estate business that serves you and your family. In the next chapter, we go into more detail about our Associate Programs and how they are changing families' lives. Buckle in

*chapter 8*

# SIMPLE, PROVEN, PREDICTABLE, AND PROFITABLE WITH THE RIGHT COACH

I have referred several times to my coaching new investors. This chapter will explain in detail how that coaching works and how it provides investors a simple, proven, predictable, and profitable game plan.

But being coachable involves a lot more than signing up for a program. Being a transaction engineer requires not only learning types of deals but also developing the right work habits. To help you understand what I mean, let's go back to where the book began: the 2008 debacle when we were out of money and dealing with multiple property foreclosures and workouts. We got back on track to succeed using six techniques that I will share with you here.

There's a very, very important mental and psychological component that we've added to all our training with our Associates. There are one-on-one and group coaching options directly with one of our own coaches. You can find more information at **smartrealestatecoach.com/nfa**.

## 1. THE RIGHT COACH

The first way we were able to reengineer our business was by finding several people who already had done exactly what we were thinking of doing. We added resources to that, meaning online and other study material. We basically did what I've always advocated—identified the path (niche) we wanted to take and then connected with someone who could lead us with mentoring and coaching. In our case, we then did something that the industry has not provided yet—created systems and support around the TERMS business to ensure success.

*Anyone attaining outstanding achievements must have motivation and persistence—but it takes coaches and mentors to keep a successful individual on track.*

Mentors or coaches (there's a big difference, in my opinion) would have to be alongside us to provide the emotional strength one needs to succeed in any business, and also feedback to keep us on the right path. Anyone attaining outstanding achievements must have motivation and persistence—but it takes coaches and mentors to keep a successful individual on track.

I'm not sure how many of you reading this book have a coach or have even thought about having one. Since I got into real estate in 1995, I have had a coach, sometimes even two or three at a time, because different coaches can combine personal, physical, nutritional, and business and marketing guidance. I don't remember a time since 1995 when I wasn't paying from $200 to $5,000 a month for particular programs. Even while still rebuilding my business, I was part of an eight-person mastermind group in 2015 that cost $25,000 for three meetings yearly. That may seem crazy to some readers, but I can directly attribute well over $100,000 in income to those meetings. My reality is that proper associations enable us to learn and profit in the multi-millions of dollars.

When choosing a mentor, make sure that person has some history of success and is not just speaking and writing but is actually doing what you want to do every day. I've looked back at my coaches and realized that many of them had had some failures in their businesses—but those setbacks significantly strengthened their ability to succeed. And obviously that improves their ability to coach and help others succeed.

At Smart Real Estate Coach, we have one program whereby we're mentoring in a group setting once a week. In all of our other programs, we're hands-on coaches in the trenches with our students.

**MASTERMIND GROUP:**

A group of people with like-minded goals who support each other and keep each other accountable in developing their personal and business skills. The concept is that putting two or more minds together will exceed the productivity of the number participating because of the ideas that flow from the interaction. The concept has roots in one of the all-time best-selling business books, *Think and Grow Rich,* by Napoleon Hill (1937).

*When choosing a mentor, make sure that person has some history of success and is not just speaking and writing but is actually doing what you want to do every day.*

## 2. THE IMPORTANCE OF DISCIPLINE

We always told our kids growing up that with the right discipline, they could be outstanding at anything they wanted, whether that be school or work. So the question is: What new disciplines could you start acting on to improve your business or your life? With daily disciplines, an idea we introduced in chapter 5, you can be improving every single day, because what you do today has a direct relationship with the results you get tomorrow.

The dictionary definition of *discipline* is an activity, exercise, or regimen that develops or improves a skill. But here we are referring more specifically to the things you know you should be doing daily—even when you don't feel like it, and even when you don't see immediate results. Among successful people—not just in real estate but elsewhere—the common factor is that they form daily disciplines that people who fail don't like to practice. In our business, one discipline can be keeping a chart of calls made to prospects each day, or whatever might support your goal or fit into your Business Game Plan. We help you develop disciplines that will support your goals.

Since the writing of the original book, we have put into place one of the most valuable tools for our Wicked Smart Community—Slack. In Slack there are numerous channels for our community to interact on. One of the many things we do in the High 6 Channel (one of the levels of Associate) as well as the Immersion Channel (another Associate Level) is post our daily metrics—calls made, appointments set, appointments gone on, contracts signed, and deals sold. Then we add—what is the one WIN for the day. This takes discipline, sure, but it's also built-in group accountability.

Reading and working on your mind can be a daily discipline, but too often the people I coach make it a goal that is too daunting.

They say something like, "I'm going to read a book a month." But if it has been months since they read a book, they should start with a simple step like, "I'm going to read five minutes a day" and then start to raise the bar as they move along. With all the aps now, like Audible, you can actually get through two to ten times what you used to be able to reading a physical book. For example, I still like the physical books when relaxing on the deck at my house overlooking the ocean or in front of my fireplace. At the gym, I prefer listening via Audible while working out on the treadmill or elliptical machine but reading a physical book while on the stationary bike.

Another idea is to keep a journal and answer these three questions at the end of each day:

1. "What's the best thing that happened today? (Wins)" I was doing some coaching recently with Jairek Robbins (yes, Tony's son—really cool relationship we've developed), and at the start of each of our calls, he would ask, "What were your three biggest WINS for the last two weeks?"

2. "What was the most challenging thing that happened today?" In my calls with Jairek, we would start (after the three wins) with the biggest challenge that I'd like to work on.

3. "How can I improve tomorrow?"

By doing this, we're constantly working on disciplines, inching forward in short steps. Too few people realize that success is within their reach, but they're just not there yet mentally. Your success will be determined by your daily agenda. It's that simple. Forming new disciplines and habits may sound like a lot of work; however, it sure is a lot easier than letting all kinds of things you didn't do accumulate and then trying to tackle them all at once. Don't be looking back at what you should have done and be "shoulding" all over yourself, as Tony Robbins, the best-selling author and business strategist, likes to say. Instead, as a result of your new daily disciplines, you can say, "I'm so glad I did that."

## 3. CREATING MORE TIME IN YOUR DAY

Here, in no particular order, are ten ways to create more time in your day:

1.  Literally buy time by hiring people to do things for you. This is the same as we explained in chapter 5 about getting a great rate of return by using personal assistants or adding team members. In our Slack platform recently, one of our High 6 Associates and certified coaches posted this for the Wicked Smart Community:

    > *@everyone: So, I was watching a webinar this morning, and someone made a point that finally struck a chord with me.*
    >
    > *Our average deal (across the board) is about $75,000. Assuming you spend an entire forty-hour week total on the deal (and most of us don't), that makes us a $1750 PER HOUR employee.*
    >
    > *But we don't want to pay a $20-per-hour employee. WTF*
    > *…*
    >
    > *What the financials are we thinking? (Says @Chris.Pre SREC to @Link)*

    I have a terrific resource for you that we personally use. As a reminder, we don't introduce people to our community whom we don't personally work with. We have an amazing executive assistant on our team now whom Zach and I both work with, and by the time this revised edition comes out, we'll probably have another. They will find, interview, vet, and help you choose the very best fit. Check it out at **smartrealestatecoach.com/greatassistant**.

2.  Outsource tasks to vendors when you can pay someone much less than what your time is worth and you also know the return on investment is three to ten times what you're paying. If you think about your income—or income goals—in annual sums, figure out what it comes to per month, week, and hour. Everyone figures it a little differently, depending on how much time they plan to take off during a given year. Someone earning $100,000 a year is making about $50 an hour based on eight-hour days.

    Considering no one can do high-payoff activities every hour of every day, any wasted high-value hours could easily cost $150.

3.  Every night, spend fifteen minutes planning, and jot down five or six priority items for the next day. This activity does wonders, helping put your subconscious to work and clearing your mind so you can sleep calmly. You'll come to work fresh, and you will stay focused all day.

4.  If you want something done, block out time on your calendar. Make an appointment to do your daily disciplines and high-payoff activities. If you know you have to make three calls, treat it like a doctor's appointment and don't let anything else interfere. It's an appointment with yourself, and it's the most important one you can have. If someone asks you to be somewhere or do something and you know you have your time blocked out to make calls, tell them you're booked. When you are doing outgoing calls, it is not a time to accept incoming calls. Figuratively speaking, you close the chamber door and don't open it until you've

completed that task or appointment. When time blocking, you're working in sealed-off chambers.

Most of our team members have moved away from to-do lists and now use the calendar. So if it's in the calendar, it gets done. If not, it doesn't.

5. Create a schedule you actually enjoy—one that you love. Don't be afraid to modify it every single month. We do that as a team. Every month we meet and see what can be tweaked. For example, I'm most effective at calling people in the morning. My son-in-law, Zach, does most of his calls in the late afternoon. That's what works for him. Certain days for me and certain hours are interviews on others' radio shows and podcasts that I've been invited on; other days are for guests to be interviewed on our podcast.

   By the way, check out our In the Media tab at **smartrealestatecoach.com** for all the interviews we've done—pretty cool stuff—and be sure to subscribe to our podcast at **smartrealestatecoachpodcast.com**. We release two episodes every week.

   Your schedule also should support your goals. Once you establish your goals, we can help you establish a precise schedule that will get them done. That's why we call the program predictable. It's not vague or ambiguous in any way. It's sort of like … if A, then B.

6. Work like you're going on vacation tomorrow. It's a neat exercise to try because we get a whole bunch more done right before we go away, whether it is for business or pleasure. Imagine how much you would get done if I

called you on a Sunday and said, "We're leaving tomorrow morning for Grand Cayman, and you've got to be ready." As I write this, I am working feverishly and efficiently because I know I'm leaving for a trip. By the way, you know you have a business and not a job when you actually can go away and things continue with or without you. When we go to Grand Cayman for two or three weeks at a time, we totally shut down. I hope you're planning at least a few getaways every year. Heck, it's only one deal or so per year—not even.

7. A simple but very effective technique over time is to go to bed earlier so you can get up earlier. One half hour times 220 workdays equals 110 hours, or almost three workweeks a year you just created. How about if you give half of those hours to your family and half to your business?

8. Spend 80 percent of your time on marketing, prospecting, and other activities to create business and only 20 percent on servicing and minutiae. To accomplish this, you must track what you do during the week, a scary exercise that may show you are not necessarily doing what any business must do to grow—high-payoff activities.

9. Start your week on Sunday night by planning the entire week, as my team does. You'll be able to prioritize and get off to a better start Monday morning, a time many people waste because it takes them until the afternoon to reset.

10. Start your month by planning it out. A couple of days prior to month's end but certainly no later than the last day of the month, look at the activities ahead, set your expectations, and set your checkpoints and accountability, which is the

next issue we'll discuss. Every month as a team, we meet to discuss the month's results and any necessary adjustments needed, and then we set goals for the following month.

We follow these up and track them at our weekly huddle sessions. We have learned so much from being part of Elite Entrepreneur, and our Mission, Purpose, Values, and meeting flow are all a result of their teachings and quarterly meetings we attend. This is not a suggestion. In my opinion, it's a must. If your business is currently doing less than $1 million in gross revenue, head on over to **smartrealestatecoach.com/growwithelite** and learn more. If you're doing over $1 million or plan to within the next six months, head over to **smartrealestatecoach.com/elite**, and we'll hopefully see you at the next quarterly meeting. Thanks to Brett and Stephanie for the amazing work they do there.

## 4. CREATING MORE ACCOUNTABILITY

Regardless of what stage you're at in business, you can take steps to create more accountability. Here are ten ideas:

1. Even if you have no boss because you work for yourself, you can be accountable to your family or significant other. When our kids were younger, we'd promise them rewards based on our business calls per day. You can bet that if you promise kids a trip or vacation based on your call goal, they'll be asking you each day whether you made your calls.

2. Start every day at zero. If your goal is to make three calls a day, the count should start at zero regardless of whether you exceeded or fell short of the goal the previous day. By not gloating over your success the day before or getting

upset if you weren't successful, you start fresh, strong, and undistracted.

3. Display a chart. If your goals are on a chart in your home or office, your family or office partners are going to ask you about it. As in number 1 above, you are "going public" with your goals, which puts powerful emotion behind them. Just be careful going public with those who may not be in support of where you're headed. If you decide to become part of our Wicked Smart Community, we'll all help you with your accountability when you post each night. Here's an example from one of our members in one of our private Slack channels:

Daily Log 1-24-20

Dials: 12

Live sellers: 9

Appointments set: 1

Appointments done: 1

Win: Had my seller/buyer closings back to back this morning. Awesome feeling to know it's done-deal #1— yeah. Hyper focused on the next. Currently have one AO contract out for signing. Another million-dollar free-and-clear property that's deciding between an AO or a 48-month OF (deal could range anywhere from $100K–$287K) and two potential sub 2 deals ready to rock; I'm just collecting information. I also have an appointment on Sunday for a free-and-clear property that Chris is calling in on speaker phone to help me on.

Second Win: Thankful for support from SREC family, $68,000 profits!

4.     Pay your assistant—or if you don't have an assistant, pay someone else—if you don't do certain tasks you said you were going to do. This accountability is particularly effective for lead generation or prospecting when you're early on in your business. Years ago as a real estate agent/team, we had a goal of calling 125 people every day, and we'd have to pay our assistant ten dollars or twenty-five dollars if we failed. We also had a mastermind group back then in which we'd set monthly goals together and have to pay an assistant or accountability partner if goals were not achieved.

5.     Let someone shadow you. You will perform better when someone is watching you. We have people visit our office all the time from different parts of the country, and even before they arrive, their visits make us more efficient because we're busy setting up a day for them to see us at our best. How about if I flew into your market and shadowed you? You'd be surprised at what you'd get accomplished. By the way, we do that at our expense for our Immersion and High 6 Associates—we go to their market for a day or two!

6.     Pay your coach. I've already covered why having a coach is so important that I have never not had one. When you pay someone $1,000 or $2,000 a month or whatever it is you're paying, you're not only going to listen to what he or she says but be accountable for getting it done. It's crazy, but as our Associates' levels go higher and higher, the participation and success rate goes higher and higher. Heck, given the profits we can generate per deal, why

wouldn't everyone be participating and profitable at the same level?

7. Post your hourly income. Earlier in the chapter, we discussed comparing the cost of an assistant to your own hourly income or income goal. I even suggest writing your hourly income on an index card posted at your desk. Do you think it would help you stay on task—to focus on work that moves you closer to your goal—if you had a sign in front of you saying what that work should be paying you? It absolutely does. You can use hourly, daily, weekly, or monthly figures—whatever motivates and keeps you on task most effectively.

8. Post your schedule, and tell everyone about it. Similar to posting your income goal, the visual cue will do wonders for your efficiency and accountability.

9. Find accountability partners. Years ago, I had a different accountability partner, who happened to be an attorney, just for book-reading goals. We would check in every month about whether we had done our reading.

   With other partners, we'd discuss our monthly deals and why those goals were or weren't achieved and whether we were still committed to them. These days, I have had the same accountability partner every Monday morning at 8:00 a.m. EST. We jump on the phone and go through the following, and then we're off to work for the week:

   • Wins for the past week

   • AHAs for the past week

   • Losses for the past week

- Fixes for the losses or AHAs

- One main focus for the week that we want to be held accountable for

10. Put yourself in a situation where you really don't have a choice. When we reengineered the business, I could have gone out and done some other things to earn money while building the real estate terms business. Instead we jumped full force into our own business with a mentor. The "burn-your-ships" concept refers to the sixteenth-century Spanish explorer who burned his ships upon arrival in the New World to send a message to his men that they could not turn back. It's great for me to coach someone who starts by saying, "I'm going to give this all I've got" and is prepared to leave a current job by a certain date. Don't get me wrong; I don't want you burning your ships before we have a plan in place and deals getting done. We can, however, get you there by a predictable date utilizing predictable patterns of activities.

## 5. THE IMPORTANCE OF PERSISTENCE

It took years for you to become the person you are, and you can't change overnight. You can change anything you want over time, but if you're thirty years old, for example, please realize it took you thirty years to form your habits, positive and negative. So please be persistent in your efforts to change, but be patient with yourself.

Let's say I'm coaching you, and you are doing everything in your game plan that we structured for your business, and you're doing everything consistently in your personal plan. Success really is just a matter of time, and lack of patience and persistence is the biggest enemy to success. I'll see people come out of the gate strong, with everything lining up perfectly—but then they beat themselves up because success doesn't come quickly enough. Every business is going to take longer than one expects to become profitable. Here's an example: We teach you the exact number of leads you need per deal.

You then go out and get those leads in the first month—then quit because a deal wasn't done. You need time to build up those leads and build up the funnel we talk about next—you need persistence and patience.

The marketing and sales process is often visualized as a funnel. When I'm coaching, I compare it to a funnel that is eventually going to have some oil go through it. When you pour oil into a dry funnel, it takes some time for it to coat the sides, but eventually, it flows much more smoothly and quickly. When you're collecting leads and filling out property-information sheets, you're "coating the sides," and in time, some high-quality prospects will pop out of the bottom of the funnel.

Persistence involves applying what you are learning—in this book or with a coach—every day, at every chance you get. Take your old ways and liken them to a spot right in front of you; draw an imaginary line in the sand, and step over it. As a coach once explained to me, at each stage of your personal and business growth, what got you to that point will hold you back from getting to the next level.

However, you can get there with the right coach and discipline and by creating more time in your day and more accountability. We're here to help you get that accomplished.

## 6. MANAGING EXPECTATIONS

I decided to add this sixth point since the last edition of this book because we've learned one of the biggest challenges in this industry is mismanaged expectations. Here's what I expect once you decide to work with us:

You did your due diligence and decided that our TERMS niche is for you. You decided that we're a fit for you because of our family, our company values, and our Wicked Smart Community. The last piece is you committing for thirty-six months. I am not saying it will take you thirty-six months to do your first deal. What I am saying is that I want you to be fully committed for thirty-six months. When you do that and listen to everything we say and follow our lead, you'll have an amazing experience. It's the individuals who say, "I'll try it …" who quit if they don't make hundreds of thousands in their first few months. In their defense, we have all seen the late-night infomercials and seminars claiming that that's possible. IT'S NOT! I'll only tell you reality, and our style as a team tends to be very blunt and to the point—it's one of our five core values, actually. If that resonates with you, let's get to work together. If not, you can follow the next shiny object and the next false expectation someone plants in you.

I mentioned our core values, and I also referenced our Purpose above without explaining either.

**Our Purpose:**
To empower individuals and families to live the life of their dreams.

**Five Core Values:**

We are clear, blunt, and to the point—no gray area.

We conduct all transactions with the highest integrity.

We constantly innovate and improve.

TEAM over me.

We match effort for effort.

We actually make decisions, hire, fire, and accept students based on these values.

## HOW WE CAN HELP

I'm big on FREE due diligence, so in addition to this book, we have several free e-books on our website, **smartrealestatecoach.com**.

- We currently have a free content-rich webinar running three or four times a week at **smartrealestatecoach.com/ webinar** (it actually comes with some amazing free gifts just for attending and completing).

- We have a full Quantum Leap Systems (QLS) Home Study Course, which has ten modules that are packed with over ninety different steps including video, audio, written, case studies, and more. This course is unlike anything to date in the industry because (a) there's no continuity fee, just a one-time fee, and (b) we constantly update it as policies, market conditions, agreements, and our internal buying and selling change. You are truly on the cutting edge and can own this as long as you and I are in business! For more details, go to **smartrealestatecoach.com/qls**.

- Be sure to attend our Double Down Sit Downs, hosted on the first and second Thursday of the month.

- Be sure to attend our monthly Wicked Smart Sit Downs (hosted every third Thursday of the month) when you can join us on Zoom (currently) with your questions, deals, and more, one hour each month—FREE for QLS Home Study Course Holders.

- Be sure to attend our monthly Wicked Smart Workshop (hosted every fourth Thursday), where we present training and allow live Q&A—FREE.

- Email **support@smartrealestatecoach.com** for more details, as technology, URLs, or schedules are subject to change.

- Two annual events: (live and virtual)
  - Business Scaling Secrets: **bizscaling.com**
  - QLS Live Event: **qlslive.com**

There was a lot of mention in these chapters about Associates and different programs. You can visit our website for more details, and those are limited and by application only.

Let's think about this and recap for a minute. Earlier in the book, I showed how the 3 Paydays typically provide profits of approximately $75,000. The Associates actually do deals with us. Is there anything to really hold you back? Any business, franchise, or other cash-generating vehicle with that type of return and minimum overhead usually carries higher price tags and fees (franchises anywhere from $35,000 to $1 million and more with overrides and lifetime fees). We're not with you for life unless you want us to be. We're capped at what we can earn with you, and then you're 100 percent profiting on your own.

Associates have access to us, our certified coaches, and all our resources, including but not limited to personal coaches, attorneys, mortgage brokers, and virtual assistants.

Obviously, everybody is going to have different results, but our Associate Programs work, and they work all over North America. You will find real-life stories about our Associates at **smartrealestatecoach.com**, and you can meet them virtually or in person at our two annual events.

When Associates are calling sellers and eventually buyers, they can lean on our fifty-plus years of experience in the real estate business. They can lean on our credibility with the Better Business Bureau, the longevity of our company, and the exposure of our website. That's a big advantage, especially in their first year in business. A really cool thing we added for them is **nationalpropertyteam.com**.

## BUILDING CASH FLOW AND WEALTH

While the ability to generate cash flow and build wealth as a transaction engineer is predictable, it's also unlimited. Since all deals are made on YOUR TERMS, you don't need to take on anything that you're not comfortable with. That means you don't have to work with any pain-in-the-butt sellers, and you can turn off the flow through the funnel at any point. If you have already booked enough Paydays to meet your needs, you can take a year off or retire. At any one point in time, we have hundreds of thousands of Payday #1 dollars scheduled to come in next year and again the year after that. We also have several million Payday #3 dollars scheduled to come in over the next three to six years. Our present monthly Payday #2s more than cover all our overhead, and we'll show you how to do the same.

That is not to impress you but rather to impress upon you that YOU can have total control over when, how, and how much you work, when you want to relax and travel with your family, and how much wealth you want to retire with.

*YOU can have total control over when, how, and how much you work, and when you want to relax and travel with your family, and how much wealth you want to retire with.*

As we reengineered our business after the 2008 debacle, my wife and I simultaneously, consciously, and drastically reduced our personal overhead by about 80 percent, or more than $45,000 a month. Without that financial pressure, we could make deals that we found fun and profitable rather than feel a need to take on just any deal. You can do the same by getting rid of any unnecessary debt or expense. I have become something of an expert at that and can help you do the same.

We go into a deal figuring out how to structure it to meet the needs of both the seller and the buyer. But then there are some decisions we make on OUR TERMS. This might involve nudging the buyer along toward a cash-out, for example, if we need more cash flow this year, this month, or this quarter. The deal could be structured from the start to allow for accelerating our Payday #3 if we know that would help us with a financial commitment. For some readers, that could be putting a child through college. Recently we had a buyer call us ready to cash out two years early, so we went back to the seller and renegotiated a little discount for ourselves in exchange for the earlier payout. Small adjustment techniques like this will add tens of thousands to your bank account— per deal! Since the original book came out, we've started to call these extra adjustments and profits Payday #4s. There are so many of these, and, along with our Associates, we are finding more and more of these in our deals. These Payday #4s drive the average per deal up even higher. They tend to be more advanced techniques and include things like the following:

- Early discounted payoffs like mentioned above. This can average $5,000–$50,000 per deal.

- "Overage" letter sent with payoffs of a SW underlying mortgage or an ST underlying mortgage, as there is always overpayment on the mortgage payoffs when rounded up and wired or mailed in. This can average $50–$2,500 per deal.

- Starting payments 60 or 90 or 120 days instead of 30 days after starting an SW term or closing on an OF deal. This means you pick up an extra two to four months of the buyers' monthly with no outgoing payment. On an average $1,500 payment, that's $3,000–$6,000 per deal.

- On deals that are contingent upon you finding your buyer, you can go back to the seller on any of these deals and renegotiate your TERMS. It's much more effective with a buyer in hand versus just in theory at the beginning of a deal. Sellers tend to jump on opportunities to move forward once you have a definitive buyer. This can be a lower monthly adding up to $600–$6,000 per year, or it could be a lump sum off of price, somewhere in the $2,500–$10,000 range.

I could keep going on these creative Payday #4s, and it's something we constantly work on with our Wicked Smart Community on our weekly live calls and in private mastermind meetings.

The cash-out from buyers is usually predictable because of their prequalification to have their credit up to standards before our exit date. So we're always setting them up to succeed. Still, we check in with them to make sure they're going to be mortgage ready, and we walk them through that process. Delaying a cash-out for a buyer might even make sense for an investor who wants to put off the income into the next year for tax-saving purposes.

*With good work habits— discipline, more time, accountability, persistence, and the right coaching—you can have a business in which you structure simple, proven, predictable, and profitable deals to suit buyers, sellers, and your needs.*

With good work habits—discipline, more time, accountability, persistence, and the right coaching—you can have a business in which you structure simple, proven, predictable, and profitable deals to suit buyers, sellers, and your own needs.

Still, some deals should simply be avoided, as you'll see in chapter 10. Before that, I'd like you to meet one of our High 6 Associates, as well as an Authority member (those who participate in one-on-one coaching with Stephen Woessner and me, specifically geared to helping the participant become THE Authority in his or her marketplace). There is an online Authority Course as well for those not in High 6 and not able to participate in one-on-one Authority training.

# chapter 9

# FINDING SUCCESS AFTER TRAGEDY—A STORY FROM A HIGH 6 ASSOCIATE

## *By Chad Heeter*

Chad is the owner of Buffalo Peak Property Solutions in Colorado and author of the upcoming book *Equity First—How to Sell Your Home in Any Market without Paying Commissions.*

In many aspects, December 25, 2017, was just another Christmas Day that my wife and I planned and prepared for our two children. Since it was also the birthday of my son, Felix, we set up the traditional "birthday table" just for him, filled with cards, hot cocoa, doughnuts, decorations, and gifts. Balloons and lights hung all around, together with a decorated tree in the corner.

Along with my son, tucked away in our small mountain cabin was my daughter, Rosalee, my wife and me, and my two mothers-in-law. (My wife, Elizabeth, was adopted, and both her adopted mother and birth mother were visiting.) Felix had finally entered double digits—ten years old! As he came out of his bedroom, sporting on his head a handmade felt birthday crown he's worn on this day since age one, we sang "Happy Birthday." Felix read aloud some of the cards sent by friends and family and unwrapped his new Xbox. Without missing a beat, we then dived into the Christmas gifts and tore off the wrapping paper with reckless abandon. Finally, I opened the last remaining present—a Star Wars T-shirt from my kids.

Wow. We had pulled it off—another smashing birthday/ Christmas combination!

Elizabeth and I had met at a party sixteen years earlier, and we each left that party knowing what was next. Upon returning home that night, she told her mother she had met the person she was going to marry. I called my friend and said exactly the same thing. We were married three months later.

Elizabeth was a born artist and teacher, a gorgeous redhead of Scottish descent. She loved working with children and taught me to always kneel down to speak with little ones. We needed to be on their level, not require them to constantly look up to communicate with adults.

Before having children, we completed our graduate studies, traveled, and planned our future. Mornings, sipping Earl Grey tea, we talked about retiring one day and joining the Peace Corps. Dreaming of our perfect home, we researched gardens and chicken coop designs, and a week before graduating with our master's degrees, we learned Elizabeth was pregnant with our son. As we both had grown up in divorced homes, our plan was to keep life simple.

Baby Felix didn't slow down our traveling. We continued to move around with teaching jobs and my work of documentary film-making—California, New York City, India, and the Middle East. To date, I've visited over thirty countries, twelve of those with our kids. In 2014, after I'd spent three years directing documentaries in the Middle East with Qatar Television, we returned to the United States to start something new. We settled in Indianapolis, and I started cooking while Elizabeth took up her art and teaching. We built our dream chicken coop, bought a minivan, and found our footing in midwestern suburban life. Our life felt simple and complete.

But two years into this idyllic period in our lives, Elizabeth mentioned she was worried about a lump in her breast. "It's nothing, though," we both said out loud. *Oh, shit!* is what I said to myself. But it had to be nothing. She was thirty-eight years old—slim, vibrant, and healthy in every way, it seemed.

We were wrong. It was late-stage-III breast cancer, and very soon after, stage IV.

• • •

Back in the cabin, as I crumpled up the wrapping paper in my hand, I glanced over at my wife. She appeared to be struggling to catch her breath. During this celebration, we had been moving around the hospice bed in which she lay. The bed took up much of the floor space of our living room, and this dance around her bed had become second nature over the course of the previous ten weeks.

As I moved closer to Elizabeth, her eyes glazed over in a fog. I could hear her breathing, slow. And then one final, gentle gasp.

I turned to the kids. "Felix and Rosalee," I said quietly. "Mommy just passed away."

It wasn't the Christmas Day I wanted. I wanted this moment to happen on any other day. But we don't get to choose that.

I bent down to say goodbye and give Elizabeth a kiss. Our lips touched, and I could feel the coolness that had already set in. A thousand emotions came crashing together. There was a wave of relief that this eighteen-month ordeal was over, as she finally escaped the physical ravages of breast cancer. As the wave ebbed, a profound sadness nearly knocked me to my knees. My children would go forward in life without their mother. Their beautiful, fun, playful, creative, patient, loving mother was gone.

There's no guidebook that you can turn to in order to learn to be a single dad after your wife of sixteen years has passed away. You do it by relying on family, friends, and sheer will.

While there were plenty of supportive friends and family around while Elizabeth battled breast cancer, after her passing they all seemed to slowly disperse. I imagined it made sense. We all needed some time to deal with this loss.

How did I deal with it? As soon as the kids were back in school, I sat alone at home. The local hospice chapter provided therapy once a week. I also escaped with reading and playing hours of *Call of Duty*, a video game that allowed me a virtual way to battle and destroy some pent-up emotions. It probably wasn't the best self-therapy, but it did help.

Figuring out how to be a solo parent was the most challenging aspect of my new life, especially as I went back to work, cooking for visiting school groups on the Colorado ranch where I lived and worked. Even the simplest tasks of making lunches for my kids and creating a soccer practice schedule for drop-off and pickup completely melted my brain. It took extreme effort to sit down and sort out what would have taken minutes to discuss with my wife. I realized those tiny things I discussed with my wife as I headed out the door—like who's going to pick up milk or return the library books—those things we naturally took for granted over sixteen years of marriage were now up to me to remember to do and schedule into my day. More than once I broke down in tears sitting in the driveway when I realized I had forgotten to grab eggs from the store or figure out how my son would get to his soccer game that weekend when I was scheduled to work. Ugh. Where was Elizabeth when I needed her?

My wife had been a stay-at-home mom for those ten years. She had done an amazing job raising the kids. Now it was on me to fill both roles—at least that's what I thought. I finally reached a point where I was comfortable calling and texting friends to come help in moments of need, whether making a meal or grabbing the kids from school.

Survival was day by day, week by week. My kids and I figured out how to navigate both physically and emotionally as a new family of three. We struggled, yelled, and cried through it all (and still do on occasion).

• • •

Six months later I tuned in to a real estate podcast. The podcast was called *Old Dawg's REI Network*. I thought the name was silly, but I liked host Bill Manassero's enthusiasm and approach to real estate investing. As time passed and the fog of grief began to slowly lift, I explored what life might look like moving forward. Summer camp was in full swing on our ranch. I listened to Bill's podcast and others as I prepped to feed 150 summer camp staff and campers each day.

Real estate was a natural attraction. I'd grown up in a real estate family. Both of my parents had their real estate licenses. My dad had his own mortgage broker firm for several years as well, and by the time he retired at age fifty-five, he held nearly fifty rental properties. My first job at seven years old was pulling weeds, mowing lawns, and picking up trash around those homes. As an adult, I had already owned a couple of rental properties of my own, and something finally clicked that I should look into real estate as an option to build my wealth to the next level.

There's a deep ocean of real estate books, courses, workshops, and podcasts out there. I dived into much of it, trying to figure out what kind of investing felt most comfortable and accessible—apartments, buy-and-hold single-family homes, notes? But a guest that summer on *Old Dawg's REI Network* changed the trajectory of my life. The guest was Chris Prefontaine, and from what I understood he not only had this unique way of buying and selling real estate, but he had also overcome some enormous personal and professional challenges. He seemed authentic and genuine as he spoke of his family and the desire to build a legacy for them. After years of taking online courses promising to "build a business in a weekend" taught by single twenty-somethings, I finally realized that Chris was someone I could actually relate to.

I devoured Chris's QLS Course over the next couple of weeks and then went right into the 90-Day Jump Start program. After stuttering and stammering through my first calls, I sent the recordings to Chris for feedback. He suggested I role-play with his son-in-law, Zach. It was rough, but I was determined to follow their instructions step by step.

One day it clicked that although I was selling a solution, it didn't really feel like selling in the traditional sense. I had no sales background whatsoever, so this realization allowed me to relax and push myself further. Soon after, I made the move to High 6 and had my first "taken."

Three weeks later, as my kids and I boarded a plane for the first vacation we'd had since my wife's passing, the sellers of that home asked to be released from the contract.

It took me another nine months to land another deal.

Call, email, follow up, make appointments, and repeat. That was the system Chris set up for me. But for months, no deals came to fruition. I grew more and more frustrated, especially as I saw others getting deals. I started to doubt myself and my decision to go in the direction of real estate investing. Chris and I spoke once or twice per week, and it was on one of those calls that I said, "I'm blocking myself. I'm blocking the flow of money coming to me. I can feel it." On one of our very first calls, just after I had purchased QLS, Chris had told me that my biggest challenge would likely be dealing with what was "between my ears." I hadn't necessarily gotten it then, but I got it now. The way I saw it, dealing with the loss of my wife and the weight of caring for my kids on my own had put me in a long-lasting funk. My mood certainly wasn't attracting money. I had to move beyond the funk.

Although I relied on meditation and prayer to get me through many difficult times in my life, I now started looking for ways to catapult myself out of whatever it was that was holding me back. I leaned on the Smart Real Estate community each week. Among many helpful guidelines, Chris suggested books to read and told me to make gratitude lists, review my goals, and keep pressing forward.

One day while working out and listening to the audiobook *Principles*, by Ray Dalio, I heard something that caused me to drop my weights, rewind the audio, and listen again.

Dalio said, "Many people who have had setbacks that seemed devastating at the time ended up as happy as (or even happier than) they originally were after they successfully adapted to them."

*Wow!* I thought. I could be as happy as—or even happier than—I used to be? That was the permission I needed to give myself in order to move forward.

I began to work harder at letting go of anything negative that was holding me back, visualizing a new life for me and my kids ... and forgiving myself.

My efforts finally paid off with a deal that totaled over $129,000 for all 3 Paydays!

The fog had finally lifted, but I continued to do the work. And within a few months I had three more homes under my belt.

• • •

Elizabeth had outlived the estimates of her hospice nurses by several weeks. She held out just one more day, and what better way to leave than by celebrating with family. I gently closed my wife's eyelids. We wept quietly as we gathered around her bed, holding each other close.

"Let's continue to have a happy day, Daddy," said Felix.

Hearing my son's words was both a comfort and a surprise. *Yes*, I thought, *let's continue to have a happy day, because that is exactly what Mommy would have wanted*. It's what she would have said, had she been able to.

That moment was an enormous emotional shift. Where did this wisdom come from in this ten-year-old? His words also gave me the solace that he would be all right, that he would someday find joy again.

At the moment that tragedy strikes, you grasp for any stabilizing thought available, just something that will keep you from crumbling to the ground. Our ordeal lasted over eighteen months, and throughout our trial, there were thousands upon thousands of moments of utter grief and stress, but also joy.

Yes, joy.

I never would have guessed that there could be joy. But as I experienced the deepest of sorrows over and over again, I saw the person I loved most dearly in the world fight, struggle, and finally fade away— and I realized that this trial was part of our human experience.

There was beauty in the sorrow.

That beauty reminded me that all would be well.

All would be okay.

*chapter 10*
_____

# WHAT COULD GO WRONG?

On a cold New England night in late September 2000, I got a call at two o'clock in the morning from one of my business partners in a set of rental property holdings near Holy Cross College in Worcester, Massachusetts. He said raw sewage was a foot deep in the basement of one of the homes. To head off a board-of-health condemnation that would displace our college-student tenants, we had to go over there and handle that cleanup ourselves. Not a pleasant task. (Nowadays, a management company handles our multifamily properties and deals with calls like these.) We discovered only after a repeat incident that tree roots had grown into the sewer line and caused a backup, the kind of problem you can't plan for.

Today, we no longer hold rental properties bought the traditional way with down payments and loans and no longer deal with many of the headaches associated with tenants, but that particular sewage problem could bite anyone in any country with any property, whether it's rent-to-own or not.

## WHAT OTHER GURUS REFUSE TO TELL YOU

This chapter covers a variety of issues with properties, tenants, contracts, and deal terms that most investors will never face but should know about anyway. Luckily, for most challenges that we've had, we've created systems for or modified agreements and forms to handle. These systems, agreements, or forms could be as simple as a checklist that we use in our office or during a property walkthrough or as complex as a legal portion of one of our agreements.

We've made additions and changes to our standard legal agreements with the help of our attorney to safeguard against situations we encountered—problems other gurus in our field refuse to even tell you about. Even better, we then update our QLS Home Study Program so you have access to it.

Some of the other mentors or coaches in our industry have told me point-blank that they won't talk about possible pitfalls with any particular techniques that they're teaching because they don't want to scare away any potential audience. I believe that if we don't teach you about what we've learned could go wrong, you might encounter those pitfalls and be upset that we didn't share them with you.

Frankly, some of the other mentors and coaches may not actually be aware of current challenges, because they no longer do enough deals themselves. Experience in the field is necessary because the industry changes rapidly, and we've got to change with the market, laws, and regulations. Because we are out in the field doing ten to fifteen or more deals per month, we are going to run into almost anything one can run into and pass along that information to our members.

Our agreements with sellers allow us to do a full inspection and to back away if we want to. Even when we are passing on the home and any potential headaches to the tenant-buyer, we might as well know up front if something has to be done and have the seller's address so that we don't have that come back and bite us if our buyer should default.

## LIFE EVENTS WILL HAPPEN

Aside from property problems, we have to deal with people's life events. One of our rent-to-own buyers was diagnosed with stage IV cancer and needed to find a place to live closer to her Boston hospital.

What we said was, "No problem. You take your time. You go through your treatments. You can become just a standard tenant of ours, and when the time is right for you and when you've found a place closer to your hospital, you can go ahead and move out. And just give us some notice, so that we can go ahead and resell the home." She was thrilled. We're fine. We're collecting a monthly check and eventually will fill the home with another tenant-buyer and collect another Payday #1 deposit. Meanwhile, the principal on the underlying mortgage in the seller's name is being paid down monthly.

One of our best tenant-buyers, who worked in an auto body shop, got pinned against a wall by a car and was out of work for a while. We were not going to kick the family out, although they couldn't afford the payments. We said, "Look, things happen. You're going to pay more to leave us and move than you are if we just lower your rent and weather the storm with you, and then when you're back on your feet, you can get back on your payment schedule." It was a win-win because we collected a reduced rent for six months rather than having an empty house, money that covered the underlying mortgage payment. It was winter, and nobody wants to move during the winter and during the holidays. Good communications saved them and us headaches.

Another tenant-buyer became disabled and had to leave the home, so we refilled it. These extreme life events affect roughly 2 percent to 10 percent of our deals yearly. In most cases we find even stronger buyers and get better down payments because our prescreening improves with experience.

We have seen new investors rushing to get a buyer and skipping our recommended prescreening by a credit-enhancement company that also checks criminal and sexual-harassment records. That can be a major pitfall. We've learned that if buyers are not properly pre-screened to figure out when they will be mortgage ready, and if they have not put down a large enough down payment, they are nothing more than tenants. A tenant can get into a home in most states by paying the first and last month's rent and a security deposit, at most. If that's the size of a buyer's down payment, all you have is a tenant who could easily default. Don't accept that. Follow the systems and guidelines we've outlined and you'll be happy, as will your bank account. Absent that, you have what I refer to as a glorified tenant wishing they could buy with no game plan to do so.

## THE "LIGHTER" ISSUES FROM OUR CLIENTS

As in any business, we hear concerns or excuses that we don't want to turn into stumbling blocks. If an Associate claims to be unable to find an attorney, we have referral sources, and for the higher-level Associates, our attorney will speak with your potential attorney in your area. We also have the necessary agreements and forms already done and packaged in our QLS Home Study Course. Since 2005, about $300,000-plus and many hundreds of hours have gone into preparation of our resources and education. If Associates need help finding sellers, we share our team of virtual assistants, who are trained at generating leads. If you're not an Associate, simply go to the Investor Resources section of **smartrealestatecoach.com**.

We often get asked by new investors, "What if the market drops suddenly?" All our deal structures involve significant monthly principal paydown, which protects against any downturn in the market. But the reality is that at any point, the transaction engineer can go back to the seller and renegotiate. As explained in chapter 6, the investor is not personally on the hook for any loan and retains the right to assign the lease-purchase agreement back to the seller, who in most cases doesn't want it back. In addition to that, we are doing more and more deals now with longer terms, and we are focusing more and more on subject-to and owner-financing purchases.

## BUYERS' TROUBLE GETTING A MORTGAGE

When it comes time for rent-to-own buyers to get a mortgage, we've seen two extremes: Some buyers call two years ahead of schedule and say, "We're cashing this home out," and that's a great surprise. On the other hand, occasionally we get a call from someone whose credit has improved, but not by enough for them to meet their deadline to get a mortgage at a rate they consider affordable. In the latter case, we have gone back to the seller and said, "Look, I know we had a cash-out coming up, but the buyer is super close and working really hard." And we ask for a three- or six-month extension or more.

It has happened twice in 2020, and both times the sellers agreed because they had been getting paid regularly each month and were super happy with us.

## THE BOTTOM LINE

Our business begins with the premise that we are not risking our own money in making deals on OUR TERMS. But as you have seen in this chapter, things can come up a year or more into a deal—a legal bill, a repair—that will cost some money. In our opinion, prudent business sense requires keeping a reserve fund, to which we dedicate most of our Payday #2s, the monthly spread between what we're paying a mortgage company or a seller and the income we're getting from our tenant-buyers. When a curveball gets thrown our way, we don't have to panic, because we have that reserve. You should also put a portion of your Payday #1s into a savings account. With all our entities, we use approximately 2.5 percent. You won't miss it on a deal, and you'll rest easy knowing it's in reserve.

There is nobody in our business, including any mentor I've ever paid myself, who doesn't get hit by those curveballs—because of two facts about the real estate market: it is forever changing, and more importantly, it is about dealing with people, their unpredictable behavior, and life events. So we won't ever claim to have it all figured out, but you've seen in this chapter how we use communication and problem solving to evolve the program that we teach our members and partners. We've been up front about what can go wrong, but the next chapter spotlights how great this business is most of the time—not only because of the profits waiting for you but also the tears of joy you see when you help buyers fulfill their dream of a home of their own.

# chapter 11

# BETTING ON MYSELF

## By James Heartquist

When you commit to something like starting a terms business, it's important to know your core motivation. Chris calls this your "why." My why is simple: I need to be challenged. If I'm not challenged, I'm bored. In the terms business, you get plenty of challenges. Every day, 40 percent to 90 percent of the sellers I call could tell me no. And with every single call, I have to figure out if and how to get past that answer. That's my kind of challenge!

I was already searching for a real estate mentoring program when I heard Chris on a podcast. He sounded genuine and authentic, and the terms business made sense to me, so I did a little research, talked to him, and came into his program at the 90-Day Jumpstart level. After two months, I realized I didn't know enough and needed more, so I jumped up to Associate Starter Level for twelve months. I attended the QLS Live Event in September 2019 and looked at the people doing the most deals. They were all Associates at the High Level 6. So I jumped to High 6.

At that time, I had a stable job, but it definitely didn't challenge me. I knew if I stayed, I'd never really have control of my financial future. That wasn't the life I wanted, because I'd rather bet on myself. Years earlier I'd started listening to audiobooks about personal finances and real estate—sometimes up to eight hours a night. I looked at all the professions I could move to without a college degree, and real estate was the only one where you could make a living AND have a wealth-building tool.

When I started with Chris, I gave notice at my J-O-B, even though I could have worked that second shift for months while I was building this business. To be honest, it was pretty irresponsible of me to quit the way I did, but I wanted to be all in on this terms business. Once I made the full-time commitment, it was a night-and-day change for me in a short period of time. Coming from a blue-collar background, I didn't have a lot of the skills needed in sales and business building. I had to learn from scratch to work in an environment where, as Zach always says, "It's not about what you say, it's about what they hear."

And what the seller hears is going to be so much about your mindset. To me, from a mindset point of view, success in this business is about

- consistency on a daily basis,

- having a vision,

- doing tasks that move you toward that vision, and

- holding yourself accountable.

Making the transition to being an entrepreneur also means you need your finances in order, so long before working with Chris, during the years I was listening to audiobooks, I changed my habits and got my finances in order. That's really important, because in the terms business you need a financial runway. You have to know how long you can go without making money. Part of this journey for me was figuring out how long I could survive on my savings and what skills I needed to improve upon in order to talk to sellers and buyers.

Today, those skills have grown in me exponentially. I have options because of the independence I've gained from being an entrepreneur. When you're in an employee mindset, you take what's offered. When you're an entrepreneur, you're more interested in what you can learn and what you can bring to the work and your own business. That's the transition I've made over the eighteen months with Smart Real Estate Coach. I literally feel like a different person.

When you're building a terms business, creativity is important, because every deal will be different. You have to be open to creative strategies to help people get to their goals; otherwise, there's no deal. One of my strengths is working with both sides to make sure everybody wins. For example, if a seller insists they have to get the top price, I might say, "Okay, but let's work on the monthly so I can get you that price." You have to be able to do that. I'm also pretty good at going with the flow and letting the deal work itself out. If you can't learn that, then you can end up negotiating so hard you wear the other person out.

> *When you're building a terms business, creativity is important, because every deal will be different.*

In this business, you're offering real solutions to people who genuinely need and want your help. So the most important thing you bring is honesty and integrity. And the most important ingredient to find is a supermotivated seller. You're looking for a seller who has a situation you can solve and a motivation that is strong. The hardest part of this business is finding those sellers. They're truly diamonds in the rough. Sometimes you'll find people for whom terms is a perfect fit, but they won't do it because they weren't properly educated. Our job is to help them understand their benefits. When their mind isn't there, even if the terms work for their situation, that's okay, because the motivation is just not there. And those deals will fall apart or be problematic anyway.

Right now, with so much economic uncertainty, I'm going with AO deals or asking for longer terms on any sandwich-lease or owner-financing deals. Most importantly, I'm being completely honest with sellers. You want to craft a deal that helps them and helps you. I say, "Listen, right now our average is forty-eight months as far as terms. But I don't have a crystal ball, and what I need to know is that if I have to come back in forty-eight months, look you in the eye, and say, 'Hey, I need a twelve-month extension,' you're going to be okay with it." Then, if they move forward, you've got someone you can really work with because you were 100 percent up front with them.

Sure, some people will get amnesia and forget I said that, but I'll know I said it. If I'm completely forthcoming about everything that could go wrong, then I'm at peace. There's a way to do things right, and that's all I'm interested in. If I had to lie to do real estate deals, then I'd do zero deals.

My first deal was a long time coming. I got to where I was questioning myself and the system and everything on the planet. It was a one-bedroom condo, and the seller just wanted to make the most money possible. I overpaid to give him the price he wanted, but I was able to do that because of the owner-financing structure that the Smart Real Estate Coach team teaches so beautifully. This seller made about the same monthly after his bills as if he were renting, and I was happy to be able to contribute a higher percentage to his retirement.

On the buyer side, the buyers I sold the property to are great people with a unique situation. They had an employee they loved and were looking for something for him to rent. The condo was a mile from their business, so he could walk to work, and these people bought it to rent to their employee for as long as he wanted to live there. They also put 18 percent down, which solved some of my cash flow issues at the time. What a great story about how to really create a lot of positive wins. I still stay in contact with them, and they even invited me to the housewarming party!

## TIPS

If you jump into a coaching program, stick to your mentor's script as you get started, because you don't know what you don't know. Once you learn the basics and get confidence, you'll make the message your own. I'm very literal, and I'll easily do the same five steps all the time, but that can hold me back. You don't want to sound robotic. As I got more experienced, I reworked the message to sound like me. That's important, because if the seller doesn't like you or thinks you're not honest or authentic, they're going to move on. It's all about trust.

Also, when you're new, time blocking is important. If you don't time block, then just do the work. Don't overthink it. When I started, I was way too focused on being time efficient, and that made me less efficient! So now I just focus on talking to fifty sellers a week. When I did that, my funnel started filling. I wasn't overworried about automation. On my own time, in my "free" time after making all my calls, I'd work on automating things that actually moved the dollar and revenue needle. Once I put those systems in place, it became more fun.

These times are crazy right now, so I keep tweaking my messages and paying attention to the different responses with each variation. Sometimes I'll do a Sly broadcast. Sly broadcast is one of the many techniques the coaching program taught me. It means we'll send messages that go directly into voice mail, and we get callbacks from the serious sellers only. This assures me that I'm always speaking with people who want to speak with me. I then print out the list and call each of those people who didn't call back. The follow-up is so important. This way, at least they've heard my voice. For example, you've got your first Sly, which goes out on Tuesday, and your follow-up call is Thursday or Friday. It's super personal, and they're way more likely to call back.

Right now I'm mainly focusing on getting longer terms. I only pivot to AOs if I'm confident the seller has the ability to manage the deal with the buyer if longer terms are needed, or if there just isn't enough money in the deal for me to stay in it. The AO deal structure is not my ideal, because it's usually not a lot of cash up front. It's going to be scheduled out over time, and there's a lot that can go wrong.

Finally, be sure that what you're doing aligns with your goals. If you have bigger goals than you can achieve in your current job, you'll know when the time is right to change. A lot of people get caught up in the whole "what if I quit my job and I fail?" thing. Well, then you'll get another job. In other words, your worst-case scenario is everybody else's life.

I want to thank the entire SREC team for supporting me through my entire real estate journey. Without your patience and support, I wouldn't be where I am today. I want to thank my family, Nancy, Terrance, Rylie, and my mom, for supporting me no matter what. Also, a huge shout-out to Dr. Amanda Barrientez for coaching me on my mindset. Without all of you, none of this would be possible.

For more information about Dr. Amanda, you can go to smart-**realestatecoach.com/nfa**.

# chapter 12

# DESIGN YOUR LIFESTYLE

The deal I am about to describe is not something that happens to a new investor every month, so I don't want you to get that idea. With patience and persistence, a transaction engineer eventually will run into sellers who are amazingly easy to deal with and ready to sign papers and walk away happy. We had a case in which one phone call resulted in two deals and instant cash flow. We had another deal more recently with one of our Associates (Cami and Greg) that was super positive and educated sellers on a whole new level. Let's explore their deal first.

Greg and Cami Goucher are a husband-and-wife team from Ohio who joined Smart Real Estate Coach in February 2019. Cami had a long desire to own investment real estate but wasn't sure how to go about  it after the recession and therefore never really made a move until 2019, when she found Chris on a podcast. For the last year, they have been working at their day jobs, Greg in the trucking industry and Cami as a nurse practitioner, taking care of their blended family of five kids, and growing their real estate business. They have a special message to those who give excuses for not having time to go after their dreams: there are no excuses if you want something bad enough … you will find the time … you will find a way. They love working together, and things have moved so well in their real estate business that Greg left his day job at the end of 2019 and Cami will be leaving hers in March. They have BIG goals for their real estate business this year and to change their lives as well as the lives of others.

In the terms business, we often deal with people who are first-time homeowners or buyers, or just new to the real estate world in general. It's an easy way for people to purchase a home who otherwise wouldn't be able to, and it offers homeowners a quick way to sell their house and maximize the return on their investment.

In this case, together with our Associates Greg and Cami, we worked with an Amish family to sell their home. This family had recently left their sect, and they were trying to sell their house on their own. As you can imagine, they found the learning curve to be pretty steep—they had no prior knowledge in terms of real estate or finance.

Ultimately, they were in a bind and needed someone to help them out.

Greg and Cami were able to go into their home, explain how our process works, and guarantee their house would get sold for more than they would get with a Realtor. Let's check out how it happened.

## THE THIRTY-DAY DEAL

As you can probably guess, the source for this property was a FSBO (for sale by owner). This Amish family was trying to sell their home, and they weren't having much luck. We were able to close this deal out just thirty days after our initial call to the owners.

This was a sandwich-lease purchase deal with a forty-eight-month term. As you may have noticed, we are pushing for longer and longer terms to make these deals recession resistant.

The purchase price was $192,500, and the monthly cost for the owners' mortgage was $1,335. Because this house was in a rural area, the one thing we did struggle with was the monthly rent price. In order to make a sizable spread, we'd have to charge a fairly high monthly rate.

We received a lot of resistance from potential tenant-buyers on the rent price when we initially listed the house, so we did end up lowering it in the end. Keep in mind, we had over a hundred inquiries on this property during the sixty days that it was on the market!

We settled on a monthly price of $1,561—which provides a spread of $226. Not the best we've seen, but the other Paydays more than make up for it.

Speaking of Paydays, let's get into the 3 Paydays on this deal. But first, there's one important note before we get into the numbers. The numbers below are based on twenty-five months instead of the entire forty-eight. The buyer wants to purchase the house in twenty-five months, and they're welcome to do it, but they will always have the option to take the entire forty-eight months if they need it.

So, with that said ...

Payday #1 is the down payment. In this case, we got a down payment of $17,587. Of that, $6,597 was up front, and the rest was paid in two installments, in March and October. We often do this with buyers if they're unable to pay the entire down payment up front.

After all, they're usually coming to us because they're unable to get a mortgage or purchase a house through normal means—so why should we expect them to make a massive down payment in one go?

Payday #2 is the monthly spread. At $226, this is on the lower end, but it does come out to $5,650 over the twenty-five months. If they use the full forty-eight-month term, that number would go to $10,848.

Payday #3 is the final back-end profit. We were able to sell this property for $219,900. When you subtract the purchase price and down payment, then add in the principal paydown on the house over twenty-five months, Payday #3 comes out to $32,026.

All in all, that's around $57,000 in profit on this property over twenty-five months. And if this goes for the full forty-eight-month term, you can add on another $10,000-plus to that number.

## EDUCATING AND HELPING AN ENTIRE FAMILY

The money on this deal was great, but what's even better is that we were able to help a family sell their home. One of the main reasons they wanted to work with us is simply that they trusted us. We were open and honest with them, explaining every step of the process and what they could expect. No one else was doing that!

The other part is that the owners of this house actually owed a significant amount on it. They owed $173,351, and with the price they had it on the market for ($192,500), there wasn't much room left for profit on their end.

If they had decided to go with a Realtor, this deal might have actually cost them money!

Greg and Cami were able to help them sell their house, make them more money than they would have with a Realtor, and educate them about the world of real estate—all while making a nice 3 Paydays!

This deal changed this family's lives for years to come …

And THAT is why the terms business is unlike anything else in real estate, and that's also why our Mission and Purpose of helping Associates do deals (versus just selling "stuff" to investors) is unlike anything else in real estate.

## TWO FOR ONE

Now let's explore the two-for-one lead. The lead source in this example was expired listings, homes that had languished after being listed with a real estate agent. We called the owners of the property in Connecticut and found out they were moving to Florida. An out-of-state move at the end of an expired listing makes for a motivated seller—one of my favorite things to see on the property-information sheet. The property was a duplex, two attached single-family homes, which in this zoning jurisdiction had to be considered separate condominiums. The property was built in the 1990s, sparing us any structural or lead-paint issues. The only reason we could think of for why the property did not sell on the open market was a steep driveway.

We were looking at a deal in which the seller would vacate one condo, which we could fill with a tenant-buyer, and assign us the lease of the tenant who was in the other condo. We generally do not want to become landlords, but in this case we were comfortable doing so temporarily. My son-in-law, Zach, met with the seller's tenant/neighbor and found a highly disciplined military man who had been paying his rent a couple of days early each month. His lease with the seller was expiring in about eight months, at which time we could renew, convert him into a tenant-buyer, or not renew and fill the property with another rent-to-own buyer.

About ten days after we took control of the two condos, we received our first rent from the existing tenant, about $460 more than we had to pay out for the mortgage. That's immediate cash flow.

Within thirty days, the other unit, which had just been made vacant with the seller's move, sold to a great military family on a lease-purchase term of three years—more than enough time for their necessary credit enhancement. That family began paying us about $1,550 per month, which gave us a spread of almost $600 after we paid the mortgage, so now our total cash flow was $1,059.57 per month on these two attached units. One phone call to a seller with an expired listing resulted in a profit of almost $90,000 even before doing anything further with the rental side.

# TRANSACTION ENGINEER
# SUMMARY SHEET

**SOURCE OF LEAD:** EXPIRED LISTING CALL-IN HOUSE

**PURCHASE PRICE:** (A) $115,811 MORTGAGE PLUS $36,000 CASH TO SELLER AT END OF TERM

(B) $127,457 MORTGAGE PLUS $24,546 CASH TO SELLER AT END OF TERM

**BUCKET:** SW (SANDWICH LEASE-PURCHASE)

**MONTHLY PAYMENT OUT:** (A) $939.72 (B) $951

**PAYMENT TYPE:** DIRECT TO MORTGAGE COMPANY

**BUYER TERM:** (A AND B) 36 MONTHS

**SELL PRICE:** (A) DEFERRED FOR EXISTING TENANTS
(B) SOLD FOR $184,900

**MONTHLY LEASE IN:** (A) $1,400 (B) $1,550.19

**SELL TERM:** 36 MONTHS

**PAYDAY #1 DOWN PAYMENT FOR UNIT B**
$21,000     ONE-TIME

**PAYDAY #2 RENT FOR B MINUS MORTGAGE**
$21,571     SPREAD OVER 36 MONTHS

**PAYDAY #3 CASH-OUT FROM SALE OF B***
$43,900     AT END OF DEAL

### TOTAL : $86,471

*Payday #3 is calculated this way: Unit B sale price is $184,900. Subtract $24,546 cash-out to seller and $127,457 paid directly to mortgage company over thirty-six months. There is $32,897 left, but add back in about $11,000 in equity gained by paying down principal for those thirty-six months.

## WHO CAN MAKE THIS WORK?

In our training and mentoring, we encounter four types of people: There are people who see the potential but lack the confidence to start even a home-study course. I suggest they speak with us in a free fifteen-minute strategy session, which I will do for any reader of this book who requests it. Just send an email to **support@smartrealestatecoach.com**, and tell them you read in the book that you can receive a free ($750 value) Strategy Call with someone from our team or me. We can work out the roadblocks, which are mostly self-imposed, and they will have some great takeaways, whether or not they choose to work with us.

Other people understand the possibilities but are hesitant to devote any financial resources. I ask them to pretend they're seeing me onstage at a seminar, and I ask the audience, "How many can reach in their pocket and pull out a hundred-dollar bill right now?" Most wouldn't have that. But what if I said, "I will give everybody in the room five hours to go out and secure a hundred-dollar bill, and those who do, come to the front of the room and receive a matching hundred dollars." A guaranteed 100 percent return on your money would make you resourceful enough to go out and get that hundred-dollar bill. We have suggestions online, including not just going to relatives or friends but discovering how to find a business line-of-credit company and how to finance with us.

Some people see the potential, have the confidence, and gather the resources, but they unrealistically expect immediate results. We teach that it might take going through as many as thirty-five leads to get a cash-in-hand deal. The people we're speaking of here go through thirty-five leads, and then they throw their arms up and say, "Well, this didn't work for me." But with their funnel of leads filling up, if they simply gave it more time, it would work.

The more mature entrepreneurs we deal with have the confidence, find the resources, and display the patience to develop a successful business. They understand that some businesses aren't even profitable after two or three years. This business can potentially be profitable within the first six months, and sometimes the first sixty days. As a result, they join the higher-level Associate Programs and have huge success, like some you have seen in this book and on our site under Testimonials. I refer to these people as being Fully Positioned with us (if your area is available, you may want to apply to be an Associate).

So, those who can take our training, manage expectations, and give themselves six months or so to see the results can run this path with us quite successfully.

## CONSIDER THE ALTERNATIVES

Some people spend $35,000 to $1 million to buy a franchise that's probably not going to be profitable for a few years. They also are likely with a franchise to have a huge monthly overhead. You've seen how our type of business can cost a few hundred bucks a month. So I say, "Come on. Where else can you get a business that has the upside potential that this does?"

You might stumble a bit out of the gate. In 1995, when I first started as a real estate agent, my coach said to me, "I want you to call twelve people daily. Just twelve people." I remember literally shaking and sweating at my desk trying to get through the twelve calls. In hindsight, I see how foolish that seems now. But in 2013, when we reengineered this business, I had to create and learn a different script, a different role, and a different structure, and it wasn't easy. I remember my son-in-law, Zach, starting out brand new at the scripts, with no experience, sending me taped audio files of his calls that showed he had a long way to go before he mastered the job. Just ten months later, he had become an absolute machine with the scripts—it was his call that brought in the deal at the beginning of this chapter. Fast-forward to the writing of this revised edition, and Zach has Seller Specialists working for him on our team buying all our properties, coaches higher-level Associates all over North America, and has become an expert in the terms business. You can too.

We offer these Associate Levels in which you'll have my team and me calling on prospects with you, which will shorten your learning curve dramatically and bridge the gap between brand-new investor and master transaction engineer.

## NO SUBSTITUTE FOR EXPERIENCE

Your prospects will look at our experience and credibility. For example, one of our Associates initiated a call with a man selling a beautiful four-thousand-square-foot $525,000 Virginia home just blocks from the ocean. She had a decent conversation with the seller but felt a little unsure and told him the next step would be for him to speak with her senior Associate—me. A few days later, I spent twenty minutes on the phone with the seller, who told me he was favoring our company over a national competitor because he had checked out the Better Business Bureau rating, testimonials, and track record and liked the fact that we had a family company. That's how credibility and experience can produce a five-figure Payday. If simply having us on your team and having your credibility and national exposure on our **www.nationalpropertyteam.com** means one extra deal yearly for you, how does $45,000 to $200,000 next year sound to you?

In contrast, one of our Associates surprised us with continual inquiries. After each email, my son would ask me, "Why are they changing the system? The system works for us." And so we had a very blunt talk with that Associate, saying, "I get it that you're nervous. I get it that you're not clear on how to deal with buyers, but just follow the exact system we're talking about, right down to using the exact email response to a buyer that we give you, using the exact script on the phone system voice mails that we give you." We could see that the Associate's second-guessing had been muddying up communications and driving away buyers. Not long after our talk, the Associate made a successful first deal and received a nice, juicy Payday #1 check.

We have outlined an ideal path for new Associates, and each Associate is teamed up with one of our certified coaches and the higher levels with me and our team (as of this writing, the only people I coach one-on-one are the High 6 Associates).

We can put the lead-generation mechanisms in place to get the right number of leads from the right sources. We'll do your first few calls for you and with you and send you the recordings. Then we'll start doing some three-way phone calls together or provide recordings of follow-up to your calls. At any time in the relationship with us as an Associate, if you feel stuck, nervous, unsure of your next sentence or scripts—anything whatsoever—you simply pull back and say, "You know what? I think I've got enough information. I'm going to have one of my senior Associates give you a call." You always have that as a crutch at any stage of the business.

Keep in mind, as part of being in some of the Associate Levels, you actually have me or someone on our team or a certified coach traveling to your market and being at the homes with you. This is a game changer, and it serves well as far as closing that gap of time between starting and your first deal. All levels have access to an office visit, to be with us for two days in-office and meet sellers.

## TESTIMONIALS FROM ...

### An Office Visit (office visits are free for all Associate Levels)

*"Hey, Chris, it was absolutely amazing to be part of your team for a day. It motivated me to push forward on my business and adopt many of the strategies we discussed. Nick, Kayla, Zach, and team were great, and now I understand why you are able to close so many deals on a monthly basis: you've got a rock-solid team!"*

—Enis S.

*"We visited the SREC office last year and weren't sure what to expect for the day. We learned quickly that the entire team does exactly what they teach. We sat in with Zach while he worked with*  *sellers, Nick while he worked with buyers, and the whole team while we worked on tweaking our schedule to be more productive with the little time we had each day. That piece—dissecting our daily schedule and reorganizing activities—was a turning point in our business. We were able to make simple adjustments to maximize our time; as a result, we started getting more deals! Visiting the SREC team was incredibly helpful, and we can't wait to go back. (High 6 Associates can visit as often as necessary.)"*

—Lauren and Steve M.
*High 6 Associates, Certified Coaches, and part of Authority*

*"Having the opportunity to 'look under the hood' at the Smart Real Estate office was instrumental in putting my business on the path to success. During my visit I saw that Chris's family is*

*doing exactly as they teach—make calls, set appointments, get a deal, and repeat. In addition, they did a deep dive into my daily process and schedule in order to help me maximize my efficiency and work-life balance."*

—Chad H.

We also host private masterminds for the Immersion and High 6 Associates as part of their membership. Chris privately hosts the High 6 as of the writing of this revised edition.

## Mastermind-Group Participants

*"We have been in two mastermind groups with Chris and have already registered for the next one coming up. The knowledge, support, and encouragement we receive from being a part of this*

*group is truly invaluable and has helped us so much in our business. It's great to have the opportunity to talk with other people who are going through some of the same challenges and successes that*

*we are, and it gives us a sense of camaraderie. Chris is amazing and answers our questions and gives us education and suggestions during our group discussions … The expertise and guidance he provides is something you can't put a price on. I would pay for the entire program again just for Chris's thought leadership and experience if I had to. We just got four properties under contract in nine days thanks to Chris's help and support."*

—Jeff and Tami S., Seattle, Washington

*"I joined the SREC family a little over three years ago, and my life has changed drastically from the day I started. Not only has my knowledge and experience in real estate investing vastly improved, but my financial mindset has shifted to a world of abundance and endless possibilities. The main goal that I had when I first sought out a coach was to get to a level where I felt comfortable leaving a great-paying job to be on my own full time, controlling my own life on my terms! I recently quit my job and am a full-time real estate investor and now certified SREC Coach. All wouldn't have been possible without Chris's and his family's help. The program they have put together is second to none, and you won't find another like it out there. Learning how to buy and sell on terms has opened the RE investing world to me with minimal risk and very little competition. I have become the local expert in my area, which has given me the knowledge and confidence to put together deals on my terms. Thank you, SREC, for creating the platform to get me where I am today. I have gigantic goals planned ahead for my future, and I have no doubts about reaching them."*

—Mike M.
*High 6 Associate and Certified Coach for Smart Real Estate*

Mike is also a member of the private Authority Coaching that Chris and Stephen Woessner provide one-on-one. It helps High 6 Associates be THE Authority in their respective markets. If you're not High 6 or the cost is prohibitive for their one-on-one coaching, you can take the online course, Be the Authority, for a fraction of the cost. Find out more at **predictiveroi.com/be-the-authority**.

*"Personally, I believe commitment, integrity, and transparency are essential in any relationship. Unfortunately, in the 'fake news' and photoshopped world we live in, they are entirely too easy to claim and promote as driving forces of an organization. When I first joined SREC, I was skeptical (albeit hopeful) I would find much, if any, of what was being billed as the framework of the organization. Over two years later (and as a certified coach within the organization), I can completely attest to the fact that it is probably even more real now than it was then. This is a varied and diverse group of investors following a well-defined but flexible plan laid out by someone with many years of experience dealing with all types of real estate and*

*business challenges. Not only does he lay it out, he will also get in front of the group and transparently and openly discuss both successes and failures. WE ARE ALL active investors doing deals daily alongside Associates; some we coach, but many we are also friends with.*

*Here's a perfect example of a situation that recently (April 2020) happened with an Associate I'm coaching.*

*We had a deal we'd spent a good deal of time on and finally had a buyer lined up, and the seller got cold feet. Here is a perfect example of the transparency; I'm telling you it's not always sunshine, rainbows, and unicorns in a testimonial. The seller was getting cold feet, and Chris Pre and I discussed it and were concerned about several things: a seller who is starting out difficult to deal with, an Associate losing a hard-fought deal, and a buyer who could potentially be in jeopardy. In talking with the*

*Associate, they were frustrated with the seller but more concerned about the buyer and their possibly precarious position. In the end, after several hours of discussion and deliberation, Chris and I told the Associate that it was their deal, but our recommendation was to walk away from it. I cannot stress enough how comforting and supportive it is to have not only the SREC team but also this active group of investors by my side as I travel this life-changing journey. That's my total transparent commitment to anyone taking the time to read this testimonial."*

—Link E., North Carolina
*High 6 Associate and Certified Coach for Smart Real Estate*

*"Hard to believe it's been three whole years since I joined Chris and the SREC community. It all started with this amazing little*

*book, and the growth I've enjoyed along the way, both as a real estate investor and as an ever-evolving human being, has been nothing short of incredible. Sorry, but you CAN teach old dogs new tricks (I'm now seventy-four years young), and I can't wait to see what my next three years with SREC will bring. Read this book, because now's the best time for how we invest!"*

—Bill R., Washington, DC
*High 6 Associate*

*"One of the things that attracted us to the Smart Real Estate Coach team was their up-front, honest approach and commitment to family. We operate very much the same way, and after connecting with Chris, Zach, Nick, and Kayla, we knew this group was special and one we wanted to be part of. I can*

*confidently say our expectations have not only been met but far exceeded. SREC and the Wicked Smart Community as a whole have continually helped us grow, both personally and professionally; we have made incredible strides toward our goals with the help of this group. With the use of their tried-and-true systems, we haven't needed to reinvent the wheel. They made the mistakes so we don't have to! Getting deals is not always easy, and the support from fellow Associates and our coach has surely been a deciding factor in our success (Chris). Steve just quit his J-O-B and is doing deals full time, which was one our goals for this year! It's pretty amazing what simplicity, systems, support, and GRIT can do! We are on track to have our best year yet, again."*

—Lauren and Steve M., Connecticut
*High 6 Associates and Certified Coaches for Smart Real Estate*

*"I've known Chris and have been working with him and his team for about four years now, doing the terms business part time following his guidance and methods of investing in real estate. It's been a great experience for me and my family, and I've learned a lot and continue to learn every day and have made substantial profits doing exactly what Chris and his team do and not reinventing the wheel. He and the team have a simple plan and several key systems in place that lay the foundation to*

*massive short- and long-term wealth. His book is down to earth and full of practical information that you can easily digest and implement and that creates multiple Paydays without using your own cash or credit, resulting in a win-win for all parties. In addition, Chris has created a culture and group of like-minded investors who meet on a regular basis to share best practices and help one another, and that alone is priceless."*

—Don S., Dallas, Pennsylvania
*High 6 Associate*

*"Working with Smart Real Estate Coach has been an amazing experience. Everything from the daily support to the community interaction to the friendships made. My life has significantly improved since becoming an SREC Associate. I just want to thank Chris and the team as well as the Wicked Smart Community for always being there when I need them. Truly a special group of people."*

—James H., Boston, Massachusetts
*High 6 Associate*

*"I have had the pleasure and honor of being an Associate with Chris Prefontaine and the family team for three years. I have found Chris to be not only exceptionally experienced but also, and perhaps of even greater value, exceptionally creative. This is his natural niche, and the results that have come from his coaching and mentorship for me and the other Associates bear that out in spades. He is the quintessential transaction engineer, both in creating win-win-win deals and when the occasional pivot is required during the course of the term. Of additional great value has been his and the team's accessibility whenever needed to maximize the potential of a deal. This second edition of Real Estate on Your Terms reflects the experi-*

ences that we have all gone through in the past few years and how we can continue to create ongoing cash flow and profits for years to come. I love the layout of the book … entertaining and easy to find salient tidbits. Enjoy!"

—Claudia D., Arizona
*High 6 Associate*

"Since the release of the first edition of this book, we've created the amazing Wicked Smart Community on Slack with all our Associates. They help each other nonstop, encourage each other, and provide accountability. Associates and 90-Day Jump Start members are allowed to be part of this Slack group. It not only includes open communication but also has channels for scripts and live calls, lessons learned, Morning Coffee videos from Chris and Zach, and much more.

The Wicked Smart Community is vital to my progress as I build my business. I'm constantly learning from the Slack community, plus it's amazing (and motivating) to see others hit their goals and transform their lives."

—Chad H., Colorado
*Certified Coach and part of Authority*

"The Wicked Smart Community and Slack provide an incredible platform for knowledge sharing, support, and inspiration. It keeps me motivated and inspired on a daily basis."

—Lara M., Tennessee
*Part of Authority*

*"The Wicked Smart Community is the 'secret sauce' to learning the terms business with Chris. Put the community experience, insight, and shared learnings together with SREC's guidance, and you have what makes the system unique—real people doing the business and helping each other grow. Brilliant! While Chris was visiting my marketplace (one of the benefits of Immersion and High 6), I was asking him some questions about what he would do in certain scenarios. One single answer caused me to say, 'Now, that's why I paid for High 6—that answer right there!'"*

—Jennifer H., Arkansas
*Part of Authority*

*"The Wicked Smart Community and Slack channel have been such an integral part of my success as a real estate investor. I have recently gone full time as an investor, and without this group that SREC has put together, I would not be where I am today. Just knowing that I have the full support of the Wicked Smart Community behind me gives me the confidence to take my RE business to levels I would've never imagined."*

—Mike M., Fresno, California

### The Team Speaks in Person and Virtually to Real Estate Investment Groups All Over North America

*"Dear Chris, I very much appreciated your taking the time to make your presentation Thursday night. I'm sure it was the end of a very long day for you. The feedback I received indicated that you were clearly knowledgeable and in the real world doing the very deals you described. Your presentation maintained interest with stories, and there was good audience participation throughout. I feel the listeners gained some insights into a way of*

*doing real estate practiced by almost no one here in RI, and you made available some very valuable tools for implementing your strategies."*

—Rick C., REREIG

*"I was blown away at how professional and organized your recent online conference was. The breakout rooms were very valuable, the speakers were high level with great information, and the deal examples were extremely insightful.*

*It's amazing how quickly you transitioned from an in-person event to online—seamlessly, yet kept it interesting and interactive for two full days online. Thanks and congratulations on being a business that can 'pivot and adapt' so quickly!"*

—Kathy Gilmore, Diversified Investor Group, Philadelphia, Pennsylvania

*"Having organized and participated in many Zoom conferences over the past month, it was very interesting to see how the pros do it. I couldn't believe you kept my attention for two full days! The speakers were all very impressive, and the content was solid. However, what impressed me the most was the way your team managed the technical aspect of running the conference. The small breakout groups were seamlessly integrated throughout the two days, creating a small-group atmosphere. And you even managed to get short surveys in every day! Well done! Impossible to believe this was your first virtual conference."*

—Raymond K. Lemire, DIG (Philadelphia REIA)

## Associate on Mentorship

*"I'm a social worker by training and have only a small amount of experience in real estate investment. Chris turned out to be the perfect coach for me, as he takes me step by step through the many processes that he knows so well. Even my most basic questions are taken seriously, and I always feel like I'm getting traction and making headway week after week. I'm not floundering anymore by aimlessly and endlessly searching through real estate investment websites or other types of coaching that don't have anything to do with my goals. I now have solid plans and objectives that I am continuously meeting as long as I show up and do the work. Chris encourages me to take steps on my own when I am ready but is always there with a helping hand for when I'm unsure of what to do next. I would highly recommend Associate or 90-Day Jump Start with Chris Prefontaine and team, whether you are a beginner or have many years in the field. He has a wealth of knowledge to share and is always happy to impart it."*

—Kate M., Connecticut

## A QLS Home Study Program Member

*"I asked for and received a 10 percent down payment ($15,000). The monthly lease amount is $1,400, and the contract is for two years. I bought this house originally to flip. I paid $75,000, and I put in around $25,000 to fix it up. The purchase price is $149,900, so by the end of the deal, I will have made fifty grand over two years, plus twenty-four for the lease payments—over $83,000 in income all total. Not too bad! And all this while only accessing the membership area—super, super helpful!"*

—Laurie T., Rhode Island

# conclusion

By having regimented programs that allow new investors to take one logical step at a time to become master transaction engineers, we hope we have made it easier for those who are ready to take the next step into the rewarding business of making deals on YOUR TERMS.

It's a business in which you can be a hero to sellers and buyers who have no other recourse and earn astronomical returns without risking your own money. We've been up front in this book about the "yeah, buts" that we hear from those who are hesitant about our business model and how we've dealt with everything that can or does go wrong. We've offered to lock arms with you and walk you through your first deals, with guaranteed results.

If you have all the information you need already, go to **smart-realestatecoach.com**, schedule a strategy call, or apply for Associate Level consideration, and get ready to start. As a bonus for your having read this far, I am offering you a free fifteen-minute one-on-one strategy call with me, Zach, or one of our certified coaches. Remember earlier in the book I talked about relaxing in Grand Cayman? I'll eventually be there a lot more—or somewhere else. So visit our website to schedule your call soon.

If you are still unsure which of our programs is right for you, let us walk you through why you might choose the "middle-of-the-road" Associate Level that you'll see when you visit the site. It's called Immersion Level. We will come to your marketplace to visit sellers with you. We'll work on your setup and organization and then actually meet sellers, do some calls together, and do anything else necessary to get you cranking.

We provide your website (value approximately $10,000), and it will include every buyer and seller Q&A video that we've developed over the years and everything else we ourselves use to buy and sell.

You can participate in our private Immersion-only mastermind groups and one-hour weekly brainstorming calls with all Associates, as well as access our Wicked Smart Community via Slack. We're going to do ten deals with you and have our buyer specialist and team get involved and show you exactly how to close with every single buyer and seller. We've structured it as a win-win, where we know it's worth our time and money, but at the end of the ten deals, in which we share profits, you can be off on your own or use our coaching and mastermind groups as needed. We'll also fly you at our expense to your office visit with us. That's most of the Immersion Program. For more details, simply check out the detailed Associate Level Comparison chart. There are higher levels and lower levels of Associate, and there's even a 90-Day Jump Start group program if you're just not sure and want an affordable on-ramp to the Community.

In every market around the country, there are buyers and sellers exactly like those I have introduced throughout this book just waiting for you to make a deal with them, and I guarantee you can do it on YOUR TERMS.

# HOW TO BECOME THE AUTHORITY IN YOUR MARKET

## By Stephen Woessner

As terms deals become more prevalent, they're going to attract more attention—and more money—from large national companies that will look to enter your market and grab market share. It's going to happen. But if you've built an authority position for yourself—if you've planted your flag and claimed ownership—you'll be the one who stands out. So let's dive into the three essential elements to becoming the authority as well as some initial action steps you can take and apply right away.

### THREE ESSENTIALS TO BECOMING AN AUTHORITY

If you were asked to think of an authority on any subject, who would come to mind? What about them designates them as an authority? What's true about them? And what does someone have to do to earn and keep that title?

- They have a focused area or subject matter expertise—like doing deals on terms.

- They don't just repeat what everyone else is saying.

- They have a public presence and share their expertise.

- They don't stray from their area of expertise—think specialist (neurosurgeon at the Mayo Clinic) versus generalist (a local country doctor).

- They aren't equally attractive to everyone. In fact, they probably bore most people to tears.

- They're significant—which is different from prolific—in terms of content creation.

- They don't create any generic content that someone with far less knowledge or experience could just as easily have written.

- They're perceived as an educator in some way.

- They have a passion for their subject matter.

- They have a strong point of view, which is the foundation of all their content.

A true authority has something specific to teach us, and they want to be helpful or illuminating. This is exactly how Chris and team approach each episode of the *Smart Real Estate Coach Podcast*—what insights, tools, and techniques can be shared with the audience to help them move their real estate business forward.

A true authority is eager to share what they know because they have a genuine passion for it, and they don't fear giving away their smarts. That confidence and generosity is contagious. Their expertise is something specific groups of people (the right-fit sellers and tenant-buyers in their market) are hungry to access. You might want to call them an expert, a thought leader, an authority, a sought-after pundit, an adviser, or a specialist. They're all words for the same thing—a trusted resource who has earned that trust by demonstrating and generously sharing the depth of their specialized knowledge over and over again.

One way to recognize an authority is the ability to define them in a single sentence, like Simon Sinek. He's "the why guy." Brené Brown is "the dare-to-be-vulnerable woman." They've so narrowly and so carefully defined their expertise that we can capture it with a word or phrase. Does Simon Sinek talk about other things? Of course. But he always ties it back to his thing—the "why." Does Brené Brown write about additional topics? Absolutely. But she always deftly loops it back to being vulnerable and the power that comes from being brave enough to embrace vulnerability.

Beyond that, a true authority has a strong point of view or belief that influences how they talk about their subject area. A narrow niche, a strong point of view, and being findable in multiple places are the hallmarks of an authority position—it will help you PLANT YOUR FLAG in your market.

So let's take a closer look at each element.

## ELEMENT #1: NARROW IS GOLD

The first essential in creating an authority position is recognizing that the narrower your audience (people in your community who want to learn about terms deals), the better. It allows you to be quickly discovered and identified as someone your target audience needs to pay attention to, all because you're speaking their language. Ultimately, this means you can build an audience of the right sellers, tenant-buyers, and other influencers in your market much faster because you remained narrow. Once you've built the audience and you genuinely know them and what they need, you can be their trusted resource over and over again.

If you attempt to serve everyone as a generalist, you can still absolutely monetize a more generic position of authority (marketing expertise, for example), but if you want to get to this more quickly, you need to be ruthless in terms of focus.

It seems counterintuitive. Many so-called authorities focus on quantity in terms of audience. Many people believe they need a massive audience to hit their financial goals. But I assure you that's not true. You and your business will actually be in a much better position if you're in front of the right audience, where nearly everyone is aligned with your ideal seller and tenant-buyer avatar.

Yet when it comes time to generate leads and deals, most people want to throw out a huge net, hoping that the right species of fish will swim in so they don't go hungry. Intellectually, I get it. Yet those choices and behaviors often suggest that person is still focusing on quantity, not quality.

You don't need a million downloads to get your podcast sponsored. You don't need to speak at fifty events to have someone walk up and ask you some questions that lead to a biz dev opportunity. And you don't need to be on the best-seller list to use your book as an amazing business development tool.

Most business owners get this completely backward. They create broad, generic content as opposed to something that captures the interest of their ideal prospects. The content is fluffy and doesn't invite anyone to ask questions or lean in to learn more. But I'm telling you, when a business owner has the courage to home in on a specific audience and ignore the rest of the world (remember, one of the traits of an authority is that most people couldn't care less about their content), the audience does lean in. They do ask questions, and they will eventually put you on a short list to call when they want to sell or buy.

And when you do it exceptionally well, you will be the authority in their market—and the only one considered.

## ELEMENT #2: POINT OF VIEW

Here's what we know for sure. The world around us is experiencing change at an unfathomable rate, and it's only going to get faster. How we communicate nowadays, at best, is on the fly. But the one thing that will not change is that unique cocktail that defines our authority position. It's the combination of your narrow area of expertise (terms deals) with your strong point of view, which you apply to that area of expertise. Your point of view is what you know to be true, and it's this truth that defines how you approach terms deals and how your add value for your sellers and tenant-buyers.

For example, predictive ROI's point of view is that most business owners go about selling in the least productive, most painful way possible. They get thwarted by gatekeepers at every turn—blocked from opening doors and building relationships with their dream prospects. But becoming the authority opens biz dev opportunities without prospects ever feeling like they were a prospect.

When we layer that point of view on top of our knowledge and expertise, it's easy to see how our team can be helpful to business owners who are looking to build and scale. It demonstrates whom we serve and how to best serve them.

That's evergreen. And your real estate business should have a similar combination. You need to have an opinion about the work you do on behalf of your sellers and tenant-buyers. You need a strong point of view about your market, your audience, and how terms deals along with your market knowledge can be helpful to them.

As you fight for a seller's or buyer's attention, you must differentiate yourself. You have to plant a flag in the ground and claim ownership. You have to stand out against the sea of competitors. That authority position—your area of expertise plus your strong point of view—becomes the flag you plant. It is you laying claim to what is uniquely yours—the ability to serve a specific niche, audience, and so on because of what you know and what you believe. It holds you firmly in place no matter what else changes. It becomes part of your differentiation equation. And you need both halves of the whole.

Without the point of view, even industry-specific content becomes claimable by others. Granted, it narrows the field, but there are certainly other real estate investors in your market. If we can take your current content (blog posts, videos, podcast interviews, etc.) and swap another investor's logo for yours and no one notices, your content isn't as unique to you as you'd like.

That's what I mean by "claimable."

But don't get too finite about this. I'm not suggesting you work to create an authority position no other investor on the planet can replicate. Odds are, no matter what your authority position is, a handful of other investors could claim it as well. But that's your goal—a handful, rather than every investor out there. And the likelihood of that happening in your market is probably small. But it's all the more reason why you should immediately plant your flag.

The ideal scenario for building your authority position is one in which you have the one-two punch of a point of view (why you do what you do and whom you do it for) paired with that narrow audience or topic area (terms deals). That's a powerful combination. You can carve out a more superficial authority position with just one of the two elements, either a point of view or niche expertise, but the consequence is that if you're going to include only half of the one-two punch, you're going to share your unique position with other investors. Not awesome.

Some investors—despite the evidence—just don't want to specialize or focus on terms. They want to be the generalist investor who does some terms deals, dabbles in notes, does a couple of flips a year, and has recently started experimenting with notes. If that's you—although I strongly encourage you to reconsider that strategy—it's even more critical that you have a unique point of view. Otherwise, you risk being viewed as a completely generic choice for sellers and tenant-buyers who are looking to do a terms deal. To avoid being painted by that brush, you've got to have a distinct point of view that will genuinely differentiate you from your competitors.

You also want to make it clear that you're a generalist by choice. You're like a country doctor who takes care of people from birth to death. When you work across many options, you need to know a little bit about everything. Try building a point of view around that truth to support your generalist choice. Your point of view has to combat that "hire a specialist/authority" argument. And I will tell you, that will be an uphill climb for you. If someone has already planted a flag and you haven't, it will be a fight.

At some level, you probably already know what your point of view is, but you don't recognize it as such. Odds are you either take it for granted because you talk about it so often, or you just need to dig a little deeper to find the gold in what you're already teaching, talking about, and recommending to sellers and tenant-buyers in your market.

When you walk yourself through the triggers in this chapter and define your point of view, you're probably not going to say, "I'm shocked! I would have never guessed that's what it was!"

You just have to peel the onion back several layers to get to something that's genuinely different enough that you can own it.

## ELEMENT #3: YOU CAN'T BE A ONE-TRICK PONY

Essential number three is that an authentic authority is not a one-trick pony. What I mean is, you can't create content so narrow it works on only one channel. For example, an expert (like Chris) doesn't have just one book. Or just a podcast. You can't place all your bets on one horse (or pony, to stick with the theme).

The problem is that whatever pony you rode in on is not going to be the popular pony forever, and you can't rely on all your prospects consuming that specific channel. You need to be more findable in your market, which means you need to have your authority-positioned content in more than one place. If you're going to build this position for your business, you have to answer the question, "How does my point of view come to life across multiple channels?"

Your goal is to create the impression that you're everywhere. The good news is that it doesn't take that many channels to make that happen. You need a "cornerstone" channel and some "cobblestones."

When I say cornerstone content, what I mean is content that is big and meaty, so it can be sliced and diced into smaller pieces of content—what my team and I call cobblestones. The definition of *cornerstone* is that it's the first stone placed. When you're constructing a building, you carefully set the first stone because you know all the other stones will be set in reference to the cornerstone. When you take that cornerstone content and break it up into checklists, blog posts, videos, guest appearances on someone else's podcast, and so on, that's your cobblestone content. The combo of your niche expertise and your unique point of view should be woven into every piece of content you create. In some cases it will be overt and, in other cases, subtle. But it should always be present to some degree.

Let's take a look at Chris and the content he and his team create to help support their Wicked Smart Community. When he records an episode for his weekly podcast (cornerstone), the recording is produced and transformed into a polished episode. The audio is then transformed into a blog post (cobblestone) for the Smart Real Estate Coach website. And then the blog post is sliced and diced into a variety of social media posts (more cobblestones). Then several of the episodes (cornerstones) are transcribed and knitted together to create a downloadable e-book (cobblestone) offered on the website to further build the email list. Or some snippets of the episode recording (cornerstone) are pulled out and used for weekly content on the Smart Real Estate Coach YouTube channel (cobblestones). Each piece of cornerstone content could easily be sliced and diced into thirty, forty, or fifty pieces of smaller cobblestone content.

But why does all the slicing and dicing matter? Because people doing Google searches might land on a specific blog post (cobblestone) that references the overarching podcast episode (cornerstone) and links back to it. Each piece builds on the others, and all of them drive Smart Real Estate Coach's specific point of view.

Some "authorities" try to be everywhere, but that stretches them pretty thin—and pretty quickly. All you need are a few channels spot-on for your audience that you consistently feed with new content. You need a single cornerstone and at least two or three cobblestone channels. From there, you can use your social media channels to spotlight both.

Just remember, your cornerstone is the primary channel through which you consistently deliver useful content that is helpful to your audience. And it needs to be meaty enough that you can slice and dice it into multiple cobblestones.

Think of your cobblestones as snack-sized pieces of content (a quote graphic featuring your podcast guest, for example) that someone might stumble upon and be interested in enough that they are led to your cornerstone content (the full-length episode). You need both. But you don't need dozens.

Cornerstones, by their nature, require a much more significant time investment. Which means you don't have time to create too many. Far better to do one exceedingly well than to stretch yourself too thin, and better to be consistently present in a few places as opposed to occasionally showing up everywhere.

You want to build something you can sustain for the long haul, and unless you're going to make being an authority your full-time gig, better to start with one.

Your cornerstone content—and at least a few of your cobblestones—needs to be built on media you own and control and not on someone else's platform. That might be your website, a book you write, your own podcast, or a video series.

You can use channels like Instagram, Facebook, or Twitter to highlight your efforts, but your cornerstone content shouldn't be housed there. You don't want to go to the effort of creating content only to have some third party (like Facebook) decide to take it down or charge your audience for accessing it.

While you don't want to build your cornerstone content on a media channel that you don't own, that doesn't mean you don't want to be on other people's channels. If your cornerstone content is targeted and tied to your point of view and you're consistent in creating smaller pieces of content from that cornerstone, you're going to get noticed. That's all you need to get invited onto other people's channels. And that's rock solid awesome!

One of the key elements about being an authority is that you don't want everything to remain on your owned channels. You want to leverage other people's spheres of influence, and when you appear as a guest on their show or whatever channel they own and control, they're endorsing you, telling other people how smart you are, and introducing you to an entirely new audience.

That amplification expands your audience once you have built the foundation that earns the invites. But they will roll in, in a variety of ways.

You'll be invited to

- speak at events,

- guest on podcasts,

- write bylined articles for local and regional publications,

- sit on a panel of experts,

- serve on a board,

- write a regular column for your newspaper or business magazine,

- teach a class at the university in your community,

- be part of a webinar series, and/or

- be interviewed as a source by the local/regional media.

And that's just the tip of the iceberg.

On occasion, your cornerstone channel will shift. This shouldn't be because you're getting bored or are indecisive. It should be driven by your audience, by reactions to your efforts, by or media consumption trends. The content itself doesn't shift, but how you deliver the content might.

When I started executing this strategy for predictive ROI, my books were our cornerstone content channel. I was creating a lot of research and content for each book, and they were being published and then repurposed into articles (cobblestones) within *Inc.* magazine, Entrepreneur.com, Forbes.com, and other media. And I was then invited to guest on other business owners' channels as well as speak at events. But when my team and I launched our *Onward Nation* podcast in mid-2015, it quickly eclipsed my writing and took the cornerstone channel position. Interesting that the main cobblestones (speaking at events, guesting on other podcasts, and creating shorter pieces of written content, etc.) have remained the same. Only the cornerstone changed.

## ACTION STEPS FOR GETTING STARTED

1.  Identify your niche where you will go narrow and remain focused. Being the terms deals expert in your local/regional market is where you will most likely generate the fastest ROI.

2.  Identify your unique point of view.

3.  Decide what will be your cornerstone content. Will it be a weekly podcast, a video series, a book, a weekly column in the newspaper, or something else?

4.  Decide how you will slice and dice your cornerstone content into smaller cobblestones to protect yourself from being seen as a one-trick pony.

You will be well on your way to planting your flag—and claiming ownership—if you apply these action steps.

If you'd like to reference Stephen and Chris teaching on this topic, please visit **predictiveroi.com/be-the-authority**.

OMB NO. 2502-0265

| A. | B. TYPE OF LOAN: | | | | |
|---|---|---|---|---|---|
| **U.S. DEPARTMENT OF HOUSING & DEVELOPMENT**<br><br>**SETTLEMENT STATEMENT** | 1. ☐ FHA | 2. ☐ FmHA | 3. ☐ CONV. UNINS. | 4. ☐ VA | 5. ☐ CONV. INS. |
| | 6. FILE NUMBER:<br>25095.10001 | | | 7. LOAN NUMBER: | |
| | 8. MORTGAGE INS CASE NUMBER: | | | | |

C. NOTE: This form is furnished to give you a statement of actual settlement costs. Amounts paid to and by the settlement agent are shown.
Items marked "[POC]" were paid outside the closing; they are shown here for informational purposes and are not included in the totals.
1.0  3/98   (IRASPROPERTY.174FRANCIS.PFD/25095.10001/1)

| D. NAME AND ADDRESS OF BORROWER: | E. NAME AND ADDRESS OF SELLER: | F. NAME AND ADDRESS OF LENDER: |
|---|---|---|
| ▬▬▬▬▬ | ▬▬▬▬▬ | |
| ▬▬▬▬▬ | ▬▬▬▬▬ | |
| | ▬▬▬▬▬ | |

| G. PROPERTY LOCATION: | H. SETTLEMENT AGENT: | I. SETTLEMENT DATE: |
|---|---|---|
| ▬▬▬▬▬ | ▬▬▬▬▬ | June 2, 2016 |
| ▬▬▬▬▬ | PLACE OF SETTLEMENT | |
| ▬▬▬▬▬ | ▬▬▬▬▬ | |

| J. SUMMARY OF BORROWER'S TRANSACTION | | K. SUMMARY OF SELLER'S TRANSACTION | |
|---|---|---|---|
| **100. GROSS AMOUNT DUE FROM BORROWER:** | | **400. GROSS AMOUNT DUE TO SELLER:** | |
| 101. Contract Sales Price | 280,000.00 | 401. Contract Sales Price | 280,000.00 |
| 102. Personal Property | | 402. Personal Property | |
| 103. Settlement Charges to Borrower (Line 1400) | 2,282.00 | 403. | |
| 104. | | 404. | |
| 105. | | 405. | |
| *Adjustments For Items Paid By Seller in advance* | | *Adjustments For Items Paid By Seller in advance* | |
| 106. City/Town Taxes          to | | 406. City/Town Taxes          to | |
| 107. Sewer/Taxes          to | | 407. Sewer/Taxes          to | |
| 108. Assessments          to | | 408. Assessments          to | |
| 109. | | 409. | |
| 110. | | 410. | |
| 111. | | 411. | |
| 112. | | 412. | |
| *120. GROSS AMOUNT DUE FROM BORROWER* | 282,282.00 | *420. GROSS AMOUNT DUE TO SELLER* | 280,000.00 |
| **200. AMOUNTS PAID BY OR IN BEHALF OF BORROWER:** | | **500. REDUCTIONS IN AMOUNT DUE TO SELLER:** | |
| 201. Deposit or earnest money | 1,000.00 | 501. Excess Deposit (See Instructions) | |
| 202. Principal Amount of New Loan(s) | | 502. Settlement Charges to Seller (Line 1400) | 1,343.00 |
| 203. Existing loan(s) taken subject to | | 503. Existing loan(s) taken subject to | |
| 204. | | 504. Payoff First Mortgage | |
| 205. | | 505. Payoff Second Mortgage | |
| 206. Seller Financing | 275,800.00 | 506. Seller Financing | 275,800.00 |
| 207. | | 507. (Deposit disb. as proceeds) | |
| 208. 1A- Sec$750/Rent 6/3-6/30 | 1,380.00 | 508. 1A- Sec$750/Rent 6/3-6/30 | 1,380.00 |
| 209. 1B- Sec$700/Rent 4 mo. | 3,500.00 | 509. 1B- Sec$700/Rent 4 mo. | 3,500.00 |
| *Adjustments For Items Unpaid By Seller* | | *Adjustments For Items Unpaid By Seller* | |
| 210. City/Town Taxes    01/01/16  to  06/02/16 | 2,236.08 | 510. City/Town Taxes    01/01/16  to  06/02/16 | 2,236.08 |
| 211. Sewer/Taxes          to | | 511. Sewer/Taxes          to | |
| 212. Assessments          to | | 512. Assessments          to | |
| 213. 2A- Security | 750.00 | 513. 2A- Security | 750.00 |
| 214. 2A- Rent 6/3-6/30 | 675.00 | 514. 2A- Rent 6/3-6/30 | 675.00 |
| 215. 2B- Security | 750.00 | 515. 2B- Security | 750.00 |
| 216. 2B- Rent 6/3 - 6/30 | 675.00 | 516. 2B- Rent 6/3 - 6/30 | 675.00 |
| 217. 3A- Security and Last | 1,550.00 | 517. 3A- Security and Last | 1,550.00 |
| 218. 3A- Rent 6/3 - 6/30 | 697.50 | 518. 3A- Rent 6/3- 6/30 | 697.50 |
| 219. 3B- Rent 6/3 - 6/30 | 405.00 | 519. 3B- Rent 6/3 - 6/30 | 405.00 |
| *220. TOTAL PAID BY/FOR BORROWER* | 289,418.58 | *520. TOTAL REDUCTION AMOUNT DUE SELLER* | 289,761.58 |
| **300. CASH AT SETTLEMENT FROM/TO BORROWER:** | | **600. CASH AT SETTLEMENT TO/FROM SELLER:** | |
| 301. Gross Amount Due From Borrower (Line 120) | 282,282.00 | 601. Gross Amount Due To Seller (Line 420) | 280,000.00 |
| 302. Less Amount Paid By/For Borrower (Line 220) | ( 289,418.58) | 602. Less Reductions Due Seller (Line 520) | ( 289,761.58) |
| *303. CASH ( FROM ) ( X TO ) BORROWER* | 7,136.58 | *603. CASH ( TO ) ( X FROM ) SELLER* | 9,761.58 |

The undersigned hereby acknowledge receipt of a completed copy of pages 1&2 of this statement & any attachments referred to herein.

Borrower ▬▬▬▬▬          Seller ▬▬▬▬▬

**303. CASH TO BORROWER     7,136.58**

## L. SETTLEMENT CHARGES

| | PAID FROM BORROWER'S FUNDS AT SETTLEMENT | PAID FROM SELLER'S FUNDS AT SETTLEMENT |
|---|---|---|
| **700. TOTAL COMMISSION Based on Price** $ @ % | | |
| *Division of Commission (line 700) as Follows:* | | |
| 701. $ to | | |
| 702. $ to | | |
| 703. Commission Paid at Settlement | | |
| 704. to | | |
| **800. ITEMS PAYABLE IN CONNECTION WITH LOAN** | | |
| 801. Loan Origination Fee % to | | |
| 802. Loan Discount % to | | |
| 803. Appraisal Fee to | | |
| 804. Credit Report to | | |
| 805. Lender's Inspection Fee to | | |
| 806. Mortgage Ins. App. Fee to | | |
| 807. Assumption Fee to | | |
| 808. | | |
| 809. | | |
| 810. | | |
| 811. | | |
| **900. ITEMS REQUIRED BY LENDER TO BE PAID IN ADVANCE** | | |
| 901. Interest From to @ $ /day ( days %) | | |
| 902. Mortgage Insurance Premium for months to | | |
| 903. Hazard Insurance Premium for 1.0 years to | | |
| 904. | | |
| 905. | | |
| **1000. RESERVES DEPOSITED WITH LENDER** | | |
| 1001. Hazard Insurance @ $ per | | |
| 1002. Mortgage Insurance @ $ per | | |
| 1003. City/Town Taxes @ $ per | | |
| 1004. Sewer/Taxes @ $ per | | |
| 1005. Assessments @ $ per | | |
| 1006. @ $ per | | |
| 1007. @ $ per | | |
| 1008. Aggregate Adjustment @ $ per | | |
| **1100. TITLE CHARGES** | | |
| 1101. Settlement or Closing Fee to ▮ | 350.00 | |
| 1102. Document Preparation to ▮ | 500.00 | |
| 1103. Title Examination to ▮ | 350.00 | |
| 1104. Recording Service Fee to Sayer Regan & Thayer, LLP | 75.00 | |
| 1105. . to | | |
| 1106. . to | | |
| 1107. Attorney's Fees to | | |
| *(includes above item numbers:* ) | | |
| 1108. Title Insurance to ▮ | 775.00 | |
| *(includes above item numbers:* ) | | |
| 1109. Lender's Coverage $ | | |
| 1110. Owner's Coverage $ 280,000.00 | | |
| 1111. . | 0.00 | |
| 1112. | | |
| 1113. | | |
| **1200. GOVERNMENT RECORDING AND TRANSFER CHARGES** | | |
| 1201. Recording Fees: Deed $ 85.00; Mortgage $ 50.00; Releases $ | 135.00 | |
| 1202. City/County Tax/Stamps: Deed ; Mortgage | | |
| 1203. State Tax/Stamps: Revenue Stamps 1,288.00; Mortgage | | 1,288.00 |
| 1204. Tax Certificate Fee to ▮ | 44.00 | |
| 1205. Record Coll Assign/Memo Trust to ▮ | 53.00 | 55.00 |
| **1300. ADDITIONAL SETTLEMENT CHARGES** | | |
| 1301. Survey to | | |
| 1302. Pest Inspection to | | |
| 1303. Narragansett Bay Comm. POC | | |
| 1304. Pawtucket Water Supply POC | | |
| 1305. | | |
| **1400. TOTAL SETTLEMENT CHARGES (Enter on Lines 103, Section J and 502, Section K)** | 2,282.00 | 1,343.00 |

By signing page 1 of this statement, the signatories acknowledge receipt of a completed copy of page 2 of this two page statement.

Certified to be a true copy.

▬▬▬▬▬▬▬▬▬▬▬▬▬

For all Forms, Agreements,
Checklists and more, see
**www.smartrealestatecoach.com**
Resource Area.

## DAILY DISCIPLINES: THE POWER OF ONE

Month:

| | Frequency | 1 | 2 | 3 | 4 | 5 | 6 | 7 | 8 | 9 | 10 | 11 | 12 | 13 |
|---|---|---|---|---|---|---|---|---|---|---|---|---|---|---|
| | Goal | | | | | | | | | | | | | |
| New Contracts/ 200 monthly | | | | | | | | | | | | | | |
| FSBOS | | | | | | | | | | | | | | |
| Expireds | | | | | | | | | | | | | | |

| | | | | | | | | | | | | | | |
|---|---|---|---|---|---|---|---|---|---|---|---|---|---|---|
| Recognize Someone | | | | | | | | | | | | | | |

| | | | | | | | | | | | | | | |
|---|---|---|---|---|---|---|---|---|---|---|---|---|---|---|
| Yoga/Meditate 4x | | | | | | | | | | | | | | |
| Cardio | | | | | | | | | | | | | | |
| Run 3x | | | | | | | | | | | | | | |
| Stomach 4x | | | | | | | | | | | | | | |
| | | | | | | | | | | | | | | |

| 14 | 15 | 16 | 17 | 18 | 19 | 20 | 21 | 22 | 23 | 24 | 25 | 26 | 27 | 28 | 29 | 30 | 31 | |
|----|----|----|----|----|----|----|----|----|----|----|----|----|----|----|----|----|----|--------|
| | | | | | | | | | | | | | | | | | | Actual |
| | | | | | | | | | | | | | | | | | | |
| | | | | | | | | | | | | | | | | | | |
| | | | | | | | | | | | | | | | | | | |

# what do i do next?

We have a very simple and predictable flow for you to follow in order to shorten your learning curve and move you closer to creating 3 Paydays for yourself.

Of course, you can always visit SmartRealEstateCoach.com for our most current content. Otherwise, here's what you do:

1. **Register for our FREE webinar** for more information on doing TERMS deals by visiting: **smartrealestatecoach. com/termswebinar.**

   Plus, as a gift for reading the book and attending the webinar, book your free strategy call here: **smartrealestatecoach.com/terms.**

2. **Get started on the QLS (Quantum Leap System) Home Study Video Course** and get access to our entire online academy by visiting: **smartrealestatecoach. com/academy.**

3. **Go do deals or APPLY for one of our coaching levels** if you'd like to start creating 3 Paydays more quickly:
   - 90 Day Jump Start: **smartrealestatecoach.com/90djs**
   - Starter Associate: **smartrealestatecoach.com/starter**
   - Immersion Associate: **smartrealestatecoach.com/ immersion**
   - High 6 Associate: **smartrealestatecoach.com/high6**

# other books and resources

*The New Rules of Real Estate Investing: 24 Leading Experts Reveal Their Real Estate Secrets*
Amazon Bestselling Book by Chris Prefontaine, Nick Prefontaine, and Zachary Beach

*Instant Real Estate Investor Blueprint: The Step-By-Step Guide to Investing in Real Estate Without Using Your Own Cash or Credit*
by Chris Prefontaine, available in print or eBook formats

*Get Deals Now: Discover the Fastest and Easiest Ways to Get New Real Estate Investment Deals without Cold-Calling, Door-Knocking or Ever Being a Pushy Salesperson*
Free report by Chris Prefontaine available at: smartrealestatecoach.com/freereport

*Real Estate Investing for Women*
Amazon Bestselling Book by Moneeka Sawyer, coauthored by Chris Prefontaine

Recommended reading from the Smart Real Estate Coach team is available at: **smartrealestatecoach.com/reading/**

If you have any other questions, please email our support team at: **support@smartrealestatecoach.com.**